BISON
BOOKS

The Life of Kit Carson

Alan E. Grey

University of Nebraska Press
Lincoln and London

First Nebraska paperback printing: 2014

Library of Congress Cataloging-in-
Publication Data
Grey, Alan E.
The life of Kit Carson / Alan E. Grey.
pages   cm
Originally published: Idaho Falls ID:
Wasatch Press, c2011.
Includes bibliographical references.
ISBN 978-0-8032-6935-4 (pbk.: alk.
paper) 1. Carson, Kit, 1809–1868.
2. Pioneers—West (U.S.)—Biography.
3. Scouts (Reconnaissance)—West
(U.S.)—Biography. 4. Soldiers—West
(U.S.)—Biography. 5. West (U.S.)—
Biography. I. Title.
F592.C33G74 2014
978'.02092—dc23
[B]
2014001751

Acknowledgments

The author would like to express a deep sense of gratitude to Kelly Howell, owner and publisher of Wasatch Press. Kelly has provided invaluable assistance, and in some cases taken the lead, in the preparation of this manuscript for publication.

The author would also like to express his sincere thanks to Ms. Carlie McGinnis, Executive Director of the Kit Carson Home and Museum in Taos, New Mexico for her review of the book and pointing out certain technical errors which have since been corrected.

TABLE OF CONTENTS

Chapter 1
The Early Years

The day had dawned bleak and cold. The sky was heavily overcast and from the nip in the air the settlers were all predicting a good snowstorm before night. Lindsey Carson had just stepped outside when he heard his wife calling for him.

Rebecca was still in bed in a great deal of discomfort. In a low calm voice she said, "Lindsey, I think it's time. Have Moses fetch Mrs. Carpenter. We're going to need her before too long." Mrs. Carpenter functioned as the midwife for most of Madison County, Kentucky.

Moses was soon dressed and on his way to the barn to harness up one of the horses to the buggy for the four-mile trip to Mrs. Carpenter's cabin. No roads had been cut through the timbered bottomland where the two cabins were located. It was necessary for Moses to guide the horse and buggy through open fields and between trees when necessary. It took about two hours to cover the four miles.

When Moses arrived at the cabin, Mrs. Carpenter was outside splitting wood for the fireplace. She saw the buggy coming and put down her axe and waited. When Moses got closer he called out, "Mrs. Carpenter, Ma sure does need you right away. Can you come? I will take you to her." Mrs. Carpenter wasn't too eager to go as it was the day before Christmas and she wanted to be home with her family. However, she knew that duty called and she had to go.

Mrs. Carpenter went to the cabin and told her family where she was going. She gathered up a long woolen scarf and a pair of fur lined mittens, and was soon on her way with Moses back to the Carson Cabin. When she arrived, she went right inside to see her patient. Rebecca was lying in a corner bunk, shielded by blankets suspended with ropes. Mrs. Carpenter's first words were, "Hello Rebecca, you shore picked quite a time to bring another young-un into the world. Let's hurry and get this young-un born so I can get back to my family for Christmas." With an air of efficiency she told the oldest girl to heat up some water and get all the towels available into the curtained area where Rebecca lay.

As soon as all preparations were made, the children put on their coats and mufflers and went outside to await the arrival of their new brother or sister.

Rebecca was becoming more and more uncomfortable. Contractions were now about five minutes apart and becoming harder. In the middle of the afternoon of December 24, 1809, a loud howl came from the Carson cabin. Young Christopher Houston (Kit) Carson had just announced his arrival into the world. As soon as young Kit was cleaned up and safely in his mother's arms, Mrs. Carpenter started calling for Moses to get the buggy hitched up and to take her home. She knew she still had time to get home before Christmas.

In 1811 Lindsey Carson sold his land along Tate Creek in Madison County, Kentucky, packed up his family, and headed west. He took up land in the Boonslick area, near the center of the present State of Missouri. By this time, Kit was just learning to walk and spent most of his time with his mother around their new log cabin.

In a few years he was old enough to play with his brothers and sisters in the fields and woods around their property and along the stream that ran through it. During this time, he thought that what he was doing was just playing, but it was teaching him many skills that would become important in his later life. He was learning to identify the tracks of the different animals and to determine how long it had been since the track was made. He also developed an uncanny sense of direction. By the time he was in his teens, it would have been almost impossible to get him lost.

Kit and his older brother, Moses, were kindred spirits. Unlike their other brothers and sisters, the two boys had no desire to settle down on a farm and till the soil. They both wanted to travel and explore new territory. By the time Kit was six, Moses had him on a horse and was teaching him to ride. When he was eight, Moses was teaching him how to shoot a pistol. When Kit was big enough to hold a rifle, Moses had him out in the fields teaching him to shoot. Moses must have been a good teacher, as Kit soon became an excellent shot and was winning all of the prizes at country gatherings.

The longer Kit spent time with Moses the surer he became as to what he wanted to do. They had both heard stories of explorers, mountain men, and trappers, and Moses had decided that he wanted to explore more of the territory west of the Mississippi, while Kit had a greater interest in the mountain men and trappers.

For as long as Kit could remember, his father was out in the field clearing the land. This was a never-ending task of removing brush, trees, and rocks from the land. While Kit spent a lot of time out in the fields and woods with Moses, he was also expected to do his share of work around the farm. His job was, primarily, dragging and piling brush and tree limbs so that they could later be burned. In the fall of Kit's ninth year, he was working on a brush pile while his father was setting fire to a pile already prepared. A breeze blew a spark into some dried grass, starting a small fire. The fire soon flared up around a dead tree at the edge of the field. Kit's father tried to beat the flames out with a gunnysack, but the fire was too big for him and soon spread into the upper limbs. While Kit's father tried to beat the flames out around the base of the tree, a burning limb came crashing down and hit him in the middle of his back. Kit ran to the cabin as fast as he could, yelling, "Ma! Come quick! Pa's been hurt bad and needs your help!" When they got back to the field, Lindsey was already dead. The limb had broken his back, and a burning sharp stub of the limb had pierced his back.

Three years after the death of Lindsey Carson, Kit's mother married Joseph Martin, and both tried to hold the family together but had very little money to do it with. To help support the family, all of the children had to find work wherever they could. Therefore, Kit was never able to attend school, and thus was unable to read or write.

Chapter 2
The Santa Fe Experience

At the age of fourteen, Kit was apprenticed to David Workman, a saddle and harness maker. This, in essence, meant that he was bound to Mr. Workman for a period of seven years. It would have been illegal for him to leave Mr. Workman, who was legally free to make Kit do anything for him. Kit worked for Mr. Workman about two years and hated every minute of it. Making saddles and harnesses was not the life he desired. All Kit wanted to do was to explore and trap in the mountains to the west. However, Kit learned many valuable lessons while working with leather. Among other things, he learned how to tool leather, how to cut the leather in order to obtain the strongest strips, and above all how to tan leather. Kit had no complaint with Mr. Workman, who treated him very kindly. He spoke of him in later years as a kind and gentle man.

One morning when Kit came to work, he spotted a wagon train that had stopped by Mr. Workman's leather shop. Kit didn't waste any time seeking out the wagon master. Kit immediately asked, "Where is this here wagon train headin'?" He was told they were going to Santa Fe but had to stop for some repairs, and they were also looking for another teamster. It didn't take Kit long to convince the wagon master that he was the teamster they were looking for. When the wagon train was ready to leave, Kit ran away from David Workman and hired on with the wagon train as a teamster. Finding work on a wagon train was not easy for Kit. He was very small in stature, being only about five feet five or six inches in height and weighing only 130 pounds. Because of his small size, Kit learned early in life how to protect and take care of himself. The men on the wagon train soon learned that it was best to leave him alone. When any job came up that required extra strength or endurance, Kit was always the first to volunteer.

One can only assume that Mr. Workman was not too unhappy that Kit was fulfilling his dream when the following notice appeared in the Missouri Dispatch:

> Notice is hereby given to all persons, That Christopher Carson, a boy about 16 years old, small for his age, but thick-set; light hair, ran away from the subscriber, living in Franklin, Howard County, Missouri, to whom he had been bound to learn the saddler's trade, on or about the first of September last. He is supposed to have made his way to the upper part of the State. All persons are notified not to harbor, support, or assist said boy under the penalty of the law. One-cent reward will be given to any person who will bring back the said boy.
>
> DAVID WORKMAN

Another valuable lesson was learned on the trip to Santa Fe. Kit had demonstrated his ability with a rifle and was assigned the duty as the hunter for the wagon train. Along a small riverbed he shot an elk. He soon had it dressed out and cut up for transport back to the camp, where the wagon train had stopped for the night. The pack train party had a most welcome meal of elk meat that night and threw the rest of the meat into the back of a wagon for later use. By the second day, the meat was so spoiled that it had to be thrown out. This made the coyotes happy and taught the men that meat had to be cured before it would last. It is rather surprising that men living on the frontier were not aware of how meat had to be cared for to keep it from spoiling.

When they finally reached Santa Fe, the wagon master sold the cargo and paid off all of the men with him. Kit now had a few dollars and no prospect of another job. New Mexico was under the control of the Mexican government, and it was very concerned about all of the Americans that were coming into its territory. The Mexican government had passed many laws that limited the activities the Americans could undertake without obtaining special licenses. For example, American trappers could not work along Mexican rivers without obtaining a special license, and then any furs they got had to be sold to a Mexican trader. Mexico was very concerned that most of their furs were ending up in Saint Louis for the American trade, where higher prices were available.

Kit was in Santa Fe for only a short time when he became acquainted with a man known only as Kincaid, a fur trapper who lived in Fernandez de Taos. He took a liking to Kit and invited him to come to Taos and spend the rest of the summer there. Kit went to Taos with Kincaid and learned what he could about trapping. Beaver fur was now very important for making hats. Beaver hats were a much sought after commodity on both the European and American markets.

It wasn't too long before his money started to give out and he had to find some kind of job. He left Taos and returned to Santa Fe to try to find work. It was difficult for an American to find work as the Mexican government was trying to keep all jobs for the Mexican people. Kit finally joined a wagon train that was heading back to St. Louis.

At this point, Kit felt entirely discouraged. Less than a year before, he had left St. Louis and set out to see the world. Now he felt that he had failed, and he was returning home to confess his failure. However, when the wagon train reached the Arkansas River in what is now Kansas, they met a wagon train heading for Santa Fe. Kit left the St. Louis wagon train and hired on to the one going to Santa Fe.

Kit had an uncanny ability at picking up new languages and soon had Spanish learned to the point where he could hold conversations with the general Spanish-speaking population. Because of this ability, he found work as an interpreter on a wagon train heading into Mexico down south of Ciudad Juarez. When they arrived at their destination, Kit assisted in all negotiations for the goods they were hauling. As soon as all negotiations were complete, he collected his pay and headed back to Santa Fe.

Again, Kit felt that he had failed. He had no job and very few prospects of finding one. He did find short periods of employment acting as an interpreter for different wagon trains coming to Santa Fe from St. Louis. His longest period of employment was only a few weeks.

During his wanderings around Santa Fe he heard about a mining operation owned by Robert McKnight, who was in need of teamsters. On contacting McKnight, Kit got a job hauling copper ore from mines along the Gila River to smelters in Grant County, New Mexico. This job lasted for about five months. Kit soon decided that driving a wagonload of copper ore was not the reason he had come west. The dust from the copper ore was starting to grind into his skin, and the work was too much like working on a farm, so he returned to Santa Fe.

Kit was starting to have problems with clothes. He was still wearing the same shirt, shoes, and pants he had on when he left St. Louis almost two years earlier. His original clothing could hardly be recognized for all of the patches that had been added. On arrival in Santa Fe, Kit used his wages to buy a new set of clothes, and this was all he had to show for a year's work.

Christopher "Kit" Carson

Chapter 3
First Trip to California

Kit stayed around Santa Fe for a couple of weeks trying to find work, but nothing was available. At this point, with no work and with nothing better to do, he left for Taos. In Taos, the main topic of conversation was Ewing Young and his party, who were trying to elude the Mexican government and start trapping beaver on streams still under Mexican control. One problem the Young party did not anticipate was the Indians.

About ten days out of Taos they were attacked by a party of Indians and after a one-day battle and suffering many losses, Young and his survivors returned to Taos to try to find more men and obtain more equipment.

Kit heard about Young and immediately looked him up. He volunteered to join the Young party, which started west during August 1829.

As on the previous trip, they had to travel many miles out of their way to avoid the Mexican scouts who were watching for them to try to determine just where they were going.

As soon as they could, the Young party started traveling north. They soon ran into the same Indians who had attacked the original party. Young had all but a few of his men hidden under blankets, saddles, brush or whatever could be found. When the Indians could see only a few men around the camp they felt they had the advantage and could again attack. As soon as the Indians initiated the charge, the hidden men jumped up and started firing. The Indians were soon defeated and left.

On traveling west, Young and his men came to territory controlled by the Navajo and the Juni tribes. These Indians informed Young that when his party reached California they would find streams that were full of beaver. On hearing this, Young sent half of his party back to Taos for more traps and supplies. The other half of the party, which included Kit, was to continue on to California. The Navajo also informed Young that before he reached California he would cross a wide desert where there was no water for the men or their horses and mules.

While game was scarce, hunters for the party were able to kill three deer. While the meat was being cured, they converted the three hides into water containers for use in traveling across the desert.

As soon as all preparations were complete, the party packed their belongings and started the journey west. About two days later they came to the desert regions. As far as the eye could see there was nothing but sagebrush, grease wood, cactus and alkali dust.

The water was rationed with about one cup a day for the men and slightly more for the animals. It didn't take long to realize that the water had to be under constant guard to keep some of the men from trying to steal an extra drink.

On about the fourth day, the men looked up over a low hill to the west and saw a large lake surrounded by green grass and trees. Some of the party were ready to race to the lake, but were soon informed that what they saw was a mirage, a common sight in the desert Southwest.

About ten days into the trip across the desert, there was a sudden spurt of activity among the mules and horses. Their heads came up, and their pace quickened. They soon came to a spring fed stream where the water was clear and cold. The men found that their biggest problem was keeping the mules and horses from drinking too much too fast as this would cause the animals to bloat.

Young let the men and animals rest for a couple of days before starting again on their trip west. The stream where they had rested fed into the Colorado River, which they were able to cross without problems.

The landscape now was completely different. Instead of dry alkali dust, the hills and valleys were showing shades of green. About a week later, the Young party came to the San Gabriel Mission, which, to the men, looked like the Garden of Eden. The Mission was surrounded by gardens and vineyards, and a large herd of cattle was grazing on the nearby hills.

At the San Gabriel Mission there was one priest, a contingent of fifteen Mexican soldiers, and about two thousand Indians. In spite of the hostility between the Mexican Army and

American explorers, Young was able to get the supplies and the rest his party needed.

On leaving the San Gabriel Mission they traveled north by west to the San Fernando Mission. This Mission was about the same size as the San Gabriel Mission, but not as well tended. After a short visit, they headed north over the mountains into the Sacramento valley.

At the San Joaquin River, they found evidence of other trappers. They followed their signs until the two parties met. The other trappers were led by Peter Ogden. The two parties stayed together until they reached the Sacramento River, where they parted company.

A few days later, while the Young party was sleeping, Indians drove off many of their horses. Young immediately called for Kit and told him to pick about five men and go bring those horses back. This was exactly the type of adventure Kit had been waiting for. He picked five mountain men who were good at tracking and who had the most experience with Indians. They soon found the trail and followed it deep into the Sierra Nevada Mountains. When they finally reached the Indian encampment, Kit found them sitting around a campfire eating one of the horses they had killed. Kit and his group took the Indians completely by surprise. A good many were killed and the rest fled further into the mountains. Kit's party gathered all of the remaining horses and returned them to Young at their base camp.

Since furs have little or no value when trapped during the summer, the Young party just rested along the Sacramento River until late August. The party stayed where they were to avoid crossing the desert during the summer months with no water available for miles.

Toward the end of August, they started the return trip home -- essentially following the same route they had previously taken. On reaching the San Fernando Mission, they stopped for a short rest before proceeding on to the Pueblos dos Los Angeles. On the outskirts of Los Angeles, the party was stopped by a small detachment of the Mexican army who demanded to see their passports. When it was found that the Young party had no passports the soldiers tried to arrest them. The army soon found this to be a very poor idea. While the army was trying to decide what to do, Kit was instructed to take two men and as many riding and pack animals as he could handle and head for the San Gabriel Mission. If Young and the rest of the party did not meet them by the next day, they were to proceed on to Taos and report him dead. However, Young was able to scare the army off and did meet Kit and his group the next day.

As soon as the groups were combined, they traveled on to the Colorado River, where they trapped for about a week. At the end of that time they proceeded across the desert to the Gila River and followed that river down to the copper mines. Here they met McKnight, who allowed them to hide their furs in one of his mine pits. While the rest of the party traveled on to Taos, Young and Carson went on to Santa Fe to obtain the necessary licenses. When these were obtained, the two returned to the copper mines, where they retrieved their furs and immediately sold them on the Santa Fe market. When the furs were sold, Young and Carson left for Taos, where Young paid all of the men who had traveled with him.

Thomas Fitzpatrick
Known as "Broken Hand", he was a trapper,
trailblazer, guide, and head of the Rocky Mountain
Fur Company

Chapter 4
Trip North with Thomas Fitzpatrick

In the fall of 1831 Kit joined the Thomas Fitzpatrick party for a trip north to trap for beaver. The party traveled to the Platte River (in the future State of Colorado) and then on to the Clearwater River (in the future State of Idaho) where they started trapping. They continued up the Clearwater to its headwaters. Fitzpatrick then took the party and traveled overland to the Green river (in the future State of Wyoming) where they rested for a few days. They then traveled to Jackson Hole in Western Wyoming to a tributary of the Columbia River. (Today, this river is known as the South Fork of the Snake River.) From Jackson Hole, Fitzpatrick took the party north to the headwaters of the Salmon River.

At the Salmon River they came upon a party of men Fitzpatrick had been looking for. It was now late October so the two parties decided to settle in for the winter. During the winter several of the men were killed by Blackfoot Indians while out hunting buffalo.

The following spring, the party traveled overland to the Bear River. This river is a major stream feeding into the Great Salt Lake. The Fitzpatrick group trapped along the Bear River and tributaries of the Green River back to the main stream. Here they met another trapping party that had left Taos shortly after Fitzpatrick. Kit was informed that Captain Gaunt, a man he had met in Santa Fe, was with a party of trappers working in New Park. New Park is an area located between the eastern slope of the Rocky Mountains and the Medicine Bow Range.

On hearing where Captain Gaunt was located, Kit went to Fitzpatrick and told him he was leaving to join Captain Gaunt . Kit received his blessing and immediately started making preparations for departure. He and two others soon left to find Captain Gaunt. In less than two weeks they found Gaunt and his party on the Laramie River. Kit and his group joined them and trapped down the Laramie to the South Fork of the Platte. They then trapped down the Platte to the Arkansas River. On reaching the Arkansas, Captain Gaunt took the furs to Taos to sell and to buy the supplies that were needed. While he was gone, Kit stayed on the Arkansas and helped prepare the winter camp.

During the winter, a party of Crow Indians came at night and stole a small herd of horses. Being bothered by Indians never did sit well with Kit. Kit told Captain Gaunt he was going to pick some men and bring the horses back. He then chose five good mountain men and took out after the Indians and the horses. Kit finally caught up with the Indians and observed them dancing around a campfire celebrating their victory.

Kit waited for the Indians to retire and fall asleep. He and his men then rode into camp, gathered up their horses, and started for home. However, a camp dog felt the need to sound a welcome and started barking. This roused the Indians, and they immediately started after Kit and his party. Kit waited until they were close enough and then opened fire. A good many of the Indians were killed, and they withdrew. A short time later, they tried another attack. The second attack met with about the same success as the first. The Indians withdrew and didn't bother the group again. By the next evening all of the men and horses were safely back with Captain Gaunt.

Captain Gaunt stayed in camp for a few more days with no further trouble from the Crow Indians. Gaunt broke camp, and the group headed for the South Fork of the Platte River. On reaching the Platte, two of the men took off with three of the best horses. This really irritated Gaunt. His first action was to call for Kit, who he asked to take a few men and bring the men and horses back. Kit followed their trail back to the former camp on the Arkansas River. There the horses were found, but the men had taken the cache of furs and a canoe that had been built during the winter and had gone on downstream. Kit spent several days searching for the men but could not find them.

Giving up the search, Kit and his party took the horses and headed back to Gaunt who was still on the Platte. Gaunt was pleased with the outcome as he felt the horses were of more value than the two men whom he could no longer trust.

After a few days rest the Gaunt party traveled to South Park, and the South Fork of the Laramie River. They planned to spend the summer preparing a camp for the fall and winter trapping, but found that the beaver had been pretty well cleaned out. When very few beaver signs were found, Kit and two other trappers decided to take off on their own and see what they could do. Kit told Captain Gaunt their plans. Gaunt wished them good luck and safety during the venture.

Kit and his party immediately left for the surrounding mountains and the many streams they contained. They spent the rest of the summer looking for the best areas to start trapping that fall. Kit and his men started trapping the latter part of September and, by the first part of November, had met with very good success. They now had several hundred pounds of furs. Kit and his group decided to pack up and head for Taos. The party arrived in Taos during late November 1833. A good price was negotiated for the furs, and all enjoyed the luxuries of modern life.

James "Jim" Bridger
Mountain man, trapper, scout, and guide

Chapter 5
Second Trip North

Captain Lee, a man Kit had met in Santa Fe about 1831, was in Taos buying supplies for a trading post he and another man had recently purchased. Kit immediately joined his party when he found they were heading north in the next few days. Their destination was the Green River, where the trading post was located.

The Lee party left Taos during the last of November 1833. By the time the party reached a tributary of the Green River, snow was beginning to fall. Captain Lee decided to make winter camp and continue the trip in the spring. They had just started camp preparation when a trapping party, led by a man called Robidoux, arrived. The Robidoux party was invited to spend the winter with them.

Robidoux had a couple of Indian trackers in his party, and during the winter one of them ran off with six of the best horses. It didn't take long for Robidoux to find Kit and say, "Kit, I want you to find that thievin' Injun and bring those horses back. I don't care about the Injun. If he doesn't want to come, you know what to do."

Kit told Captain Lee what he was going to do. He selected two of the best trackers and immediately started after the Indian and the horses. It didn't take long to determine that the Indian was heading for California. After four days of hard riding, the horses of the two trackers gave out, and they couldn't go any farther. From the tracks, they knew that they were getting close, so Kit decided to go on alone.

By evening of the second day Kit arrived at the Indian's camp. When the Indian saw that Kit was alone, he decided to put up a fight. That was his big mistake. Kit shot the Indian and rode into his camp. There Kit noticed a rabbit roasting over a fire. Never being one to waste food, Kit finished cooking dinner and had a delicious meal of roast rabbit.

The next morning, Kit rounded up the horses and started back on the return trail. About seven days later he reached the winter camp. Kit explained what had happened and returned the horses to their rightful owner.

During the latter part of winter, a trapper came by and told them that Fitzpatrick and Bridger, a couple of mountain men, were in winter camp along the Snake River. In March, as soon as the snow was beginning to leave, the Lee party left their camp to find the two men. It took about two weeks to locate their camp on the Snake River.

Lee sold all of his supplies to Bridger and accepted beaver pelts for payment. While they were there, Lee and Robidoux decided to join the Fitzpatrick and Bridger parties for the spring trapping. For Kit, this was just too many people. He had visited towns with fewer people than were now gathered in that camp. It didn't take long to find four other trappers who felt the same way. Kit and a small group took their leave and headed back to the Green River and its tributaries.

They trapped for several weeks when Bridger and his party came by on their way to the Green River Rendezvous. Kit had heard a lot about these rendezvous but had never attended one of them. Kit's party pulled its traps and followed Bridger to the encampment. There were about 200 trappers encamped and more Indians than they could count.

When trappers arrive at the rendezvous, their first objective was to find traders to whom they could sell their beaver pelts. This gave them the money to buy the necessary supplies for the coming season. Supplies were such things as coffee, sugar, and blankets. It was soon found that the traders paid minimum price for the beaver pelts and charged the maximum price for their goods. The only other choice was to go without, and that wasn't even considered.

At the end of August 1834, the Rendezvous started breaking up. The trappers left in groups of about 50 men. Each group headed for its favorite trapping area. The group that Kit had joined started for Blackfoot country at the headwaters of the Missouri River. This region is located in present day Northern Montana.

It didn't take long for the men to learn that it was not wise to go out in small groups in Blackfoot country, as an Indian attack was almost certain. Indian attacks were a daily problem. The camp was soon raided, and the Blackfoot stole about 16 head of horses. This always irritated Kit, so he got about five volunteers and went after them. It didn't take long for Kit and his men to come to the Indian camp. As soon as the Indians were in sight, Kit's party opened fire. However, they were too distant to do much damage. Kit then signaled for a parley to which the Indians agreed. At the end of the parley the Indians agreed to return the horses. They said they were sorry they had taken them as they didn't want to steal from the white man. They said they thought the horses belonged to the Snake Indians. The Blackfoot soon returned five of the most broken down horses and refused to return any more. With that, the battle was back on.

During the course of the battle with the Blackfoot, a bullet grazed Kit's neck and went through his shoulder muscle. That night, no fires could be started without giving the Indians an easy target. The blood from the wound froze, and Kit spent a miserable night. The following morning the party found the Indians had not moved, but the party was too weak to continue the battle. Kit decided they should pack their gear and return to the base camp.

As soon as the party returned, Bridger came looking for Kit. He soon found him sitting by a cooking fire. He didn't waste time in asking, "Kit, how did this happen? You're the last one I thought would have this problem." Kit thought a minute then said, "Well Jim, I guess I just shot

the wrong Injun'. I saw another Injun' aiming
at Markhead and that's the Injun' I shot before
he could fire. As soon as I fired, I looked back
and saw that another Injun' I was watching
was getting ready to shoot. I didn't have time to
reload, so I started jumping around to make a
harder target to hit. I was surprised they didn't
ask me to join their tribe after watching the
dance I put on."

Jim couldn't hold back a smile, but said,
"Kit we had better get that wound cleaned
up before infection sets in." In a few days the
shoulder was as good as new, and Kit was ready
to take up normal duties around camp.

In about a week the spring trapping season
started. For several weeks the Bridger group
trapped along the Snake River. The Snake River
was too high from the spring run-off to permit
good trapping, so Bridger decided to pack up
and take his group overland to the Green River
country. There the Bridger group made a good
haul of pelts and then settled down to await the
summer rendezvous.

In a short period of time the other trappers
started to arrive and they were followed by the
traders with all of the supplies and equipment
that were needed. The pelts were sold, and
all needed supplies were purchased. When all

business was complete, the group settled down for the fun and games of summer rendezvous.

During summer rendezvous, only one problem arose. There was a big burly Frenchman named Chouinard who worked for the American Fur Company. He was the biggest bully and braggart Kit had ever seen. He was always out looking for a fight, and usually found one. This lasted until he started going around camp telling everyone that Frenchmen were good fighters, but the Americans were too weak and scared to put up a good fight

As you can imagine, this didn't set at all well with Kit. Kit mounted his horse and started looking for Chouinard. He soon found him. Kit told Chouinard that Kit Carson was the meanest baddest American in camp, and if he didn't quit his bragging Kit was going to rip his guts out. With that, Kit turned his horse and started back to his camp.

Out of the corner of his eye, Kit saw Chouinard reach for his rifle. Kit immediately turned and drew the first weapon he came to, which was a pistol. Both fired at the same time. Chouinard's bullet parted Kit's hair, while Kit's bullet shattered Chouinard's right arm. Not another word was heard from Chouinard for the rest of the summer.

About the first of September 1835, the rendezvous broke up and everyone left for the fall trapping season. The Bridger party, including Kit, trapped the Yellowstone and Big Horn Rivers, and then crossed over to the three forks of the Missouri River. The group trapped down the North Fork of the Missouri River (this could be either the Galatin or Madison river) until it reached the Snake River Country. Here they ran into another party on their way to the Mary's River. Kit had heard that the Mary's River was full of Beaver, so he joined their party. They trapped down this river until it was lost in the desert. (From the way the river is described, it is probably currently known as the Big Lost River).

At this point the party broke up, half going to Fort Walla Walla, Washington and the rest, including Kit, going to Fort Hall in Idaho. At Fort Hall Kit's party was warmly welcomed, and for the first time in over a week they had plenty to eat. Although Fort Hall was a strong fort, the Blackfoot Indians wouldn't leave the fort alone. As a precaution, all horses were corralled next to the fort. In spite of this, the Blackfoot were able to come in one night, lower the corral poles and drive off the entire herd of horses. The guards on duty thought it was some of the men taking the horses out to graze, so they never raised an alarm. A few days later, another trapping party came to the fort. They had a large stock of horses with them, so the men were able to buy the horses they needed.

The local Indians told people at the fort that a herd of buffalo was grazing nearby. A group of hunters, including Kit, rode out and soon found them. Quite a few were killed, and the meat brought back to Fort Hall. When they returned, the entire Fort and all of the local Indians had a big feast.

While out hunting there was no trouble with the Blackfoot. The reason was soon found out from a nearby camp of Crow Indians. They said that the Blackfoot had been infected with Smallpox and had gone north to escape the plague.

In a couple of weeks a large group of about 100 men, including Kit, left for the spring trapping season. With this strength, they were going to trap wherever they wanted. The group traveled north to the Yellowstone River. They trapped up the Yellowstone, Otter, and Musselshell Rivers with only fair results.

Toward the end of spring, they broke camp and all traveled to the Powder River, where winter camp was established. This was one of the coldest winters Kit had ever seen. There was so much snow that the horses could not forage for food. It was necessary to break small limbs off of the Cottonwood trees, thaw them out by the fire and give these to the horses for their winter feed. The only good thing about the winter was the buffalo. They were continually trying to come into camp and graze where the cook fires had melted the snow off the grass. Because of their close proximity, there were no problems in keeping the camp fed.

The only problems were with the Sioux Indians. They were just as belligerent as the Blackfoot had been. Men had been sent to Fort Laramie for supplies. They never returned and Kit assumed they had been killed by the Sioux.

The trappers learned that the Rendezvous of 1837 was to be held on the Wind River. When the trappers arrived, the traders were already there, so supplies were quickly obtained.

The Rendezvous only lasted for about 20 days, so the trappers were soon packed and ready to leave. The first stop for Bridger's group was Brown's Hole, where a trading post had been established. While there, Kit was offered a job as hunter for one dollar a day. He spent the rest of the winter keeping the Post supplied with meat.

That spring Kit joined Bridger and again left for the upper Missouri River country. The summer was spent along the river waiting for the fall trapping to begin. Bridger and party came back each summer to the Rendezvous on the Green River or one of its tributaries.

Kit was now seeking other types of employment. Beaver were getting scarce, and it was becoming more difficult for him to make a decent living.

During the summer of 1842, Kit joined a wagon train heading back to the States. He went to St Louis to visit friends and relatives. It didn't take long to get tired of civilized living, so he boarded a steamer heading back up the Missouri River.

John C. Fremont
Known as *The Great Pathfinder*, he was a famous
U.S. Military officer and explorer.

Chapter 6

Guiding Colonel John C. Fremont

Kit had been on the steamer for only a short time when he met Colonel John C. Fremont. Fremont had been looking for a Captain Drips who was an experienced mountaineer. He wanted Captain Drips to be his guide but was unable to find him.

Kit told Colonel Fremont that he had spent considerable time in the mountains, and that he could guide him wherever he wanted to go. Fremont said that he would check his story out and let him know. The Colonel must have done some fast checking, and the reports must have satisfied him as he looked Kit up in a few days and offered him the job as his guide.

Fremont's job was to survey South Pass and to measure some of the highest peaks in the Rocky Mountains.

Fremont and Kit disembarked from the steamer and headed directly for Fort Laramie. On their way to the Fort they met a party of trappers who told them that they had been attacked by a War Party of Sioux, and had killed several Sioux Warriors. In the meantime, the Sioux had gathered a large party of warriors and were out looking for revenge. They told Fremont that he would be much safer staying right at Fort Laramie.

Fremont had a different view of the matter. He told the trappers that he had been sent out to do a job, and a little bit of danger was not going to keep him from doing it. He further stated that should he be killed, the U.S. Army would send out troops and strike their own revenge.

The Fremont party left Fort Laramie and headed directly for South Pass. On arrival, Fremont started working and accomplished all of the duties expected of him. On completion of his duties, the group returned to Fort Laramie. During this trip, Kit functioned as both guide and hunter.

The party arrived back at Fort Laramie in the latter part of September 1842. On arrival at the fort, Kit took his leave from Colonel Fremont and returned to the States. He returned by the same route he had taken coming out a few months earlier.

In January 1843, Kit went to Bent's Fort, (located in southeast Colorado just west of Fort Lyons) and from there directly to Taos, New Mexico. At Taos, Kit met and married Señorita Josefa Jaramillo. They were married in the Guadalupe Catholic Church in Taos in February 1843. Kit bought a home in Taos, which he gave to Josefa as a wedding gift.

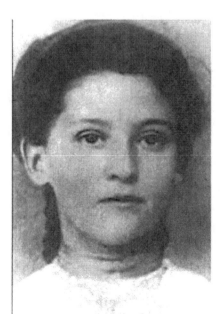

Josefa Jaramillo
Wife of Kit Carson

Kit Carson home in Taos, New Mexico

Our Lady of Guadalupe Church
Taos, New Mexico

Kit had been trapping and exploring for too many years to stay in one place for any length of time. Thus, in April, he joined a wagon train heading for St. Louis. About four days out, they came to an encampment of dragoons led by Captain Cook. Kit was informed that the dragoons were waiting for a wagon train heading east, which was being guarded by a company of Mexican soldiers. When they reached the Arkansas River, the wagon train would be met by a large contingent of Texans who were seeking revenge for the treatment their people had received when some of them had been captured by the Mexicans.

Kit was offered three hundred dollars to take a message to General Armijo in Santa Fe, asking for his help, and to bring back his reply. This was an offer he readily accepted. It took about eleven days to make the round trip. When Kit returned, he found that the trip had been unnecessary. The dragoons had met and disarmed the Texans and the problem was over.

Finding that the problem had been solved, Kit took his leave and headed for Bent's Fort. On his arrival at the fort, Kit found out that Colonel Fremont had passed through three days previously on his way west. Kit wanted a final goodbye with the Colonel, so took out after him.

Three days later Kit came to his camp. When Fremont saw him, he jumped to his feet and said, "Kit, you are sure a welcome sight. I need you again as a guide and hunter." Kit thought for a minute then replied, "Colonel, I can't think of anyone I would rather work for; I accept your offer."

They sat for a while and brought each other up to date on what they had been doing. Finally Colonel Fremont said, "Kit, there is something that I need right away. I need more pack mules. I would like for you to return to Bent's Fort, buy some, and bring them to me." Kit said, "Colonel, that job is as good as done. I will leave right away." On reaching the fort, Kit purchased ten mules. In less than a week, he rejoined Fremont on the south fork of the Platte River.

From the Platte River they traveled across South Pass and on to Soda Springs on the Bear River. At the Bear River Fremont decided to explore the Great Salt Lake. While Fremont and his party went on to the lake, Kit was sent back to Fort Hall for supplies. As soon as all needed supplies were collected, Kit and a companion departed for the Great Salt Lake to rejoin Fremont. They found him on the northern end of the lake.

The next morning, Fremont started his men east around the lake. They went about twenty miles to the eastern end where they had a good view. About fifteen miles off shore was a large island that Fremont was determined to explore. The men unpacked an India rubber boat that Fremont had brought along. In a short period of time Fremont, Kit, and four others were on their way to the island. When they arrived at the island they found a large, barren expanse of land. Luckily, they had brought fresh water for drinking and cooking since none could be found on the island.

The next morning they observed a large storm approaching. They rapidly packed the boat and headed for shore. They must have been careless during the packing because the boat had developed a leak. One person had to man the bellows constantly to keep the boat inflated. However, they reached shore ahead of the storm. In his journal, Fremont gave the Island a very appropriate name; he called it "Disappointment Island".

After leaving the Great Salt Lake, Fremont and his party traveled up the Bear River and then across to the Malad River. When they arrived there, they met up with Fitzpatrick and his party.

That evening Fremont told the group that he would like to see the mouth of the Columbia River. No one in the combined party had an objection, so the next morning the combined party started on the trip west. It took several days to cross the Utah salt flats; and then on to the Blue Mountains. After crossing the mountains they went on to the Dalles and then down the Columbia River to Fort Vancouver. Here they replenished their supplies.

For some reason known only to Fremont, he decided to turn south and head for California. In a few days they arrived at Klamath Lake and found a large village of Klamath Indians. It didn't take long to find them to be a very surly lot of people, and that the presence of white men was far from welcome.

On leaving Klamath Lake, Fremont continued south into California. This was probably the hardest part of the trip. It was necessary to cross a very desolate stretch of barren land before they reached the Sierra Nevada Mountains. Here the group ran into an entirely different problem. The ground was covered with anywhere from one to six feet of snow. It took about two weeks for the men to tramp down a trail where the horses and mules could get through. In spite of their efforts, the animals still sank into the snow up to their bellies. They had to fight for every step they took.

In order to have any food, it was found necessary to kill one of the weaker and less laden mules. It took another two weeks to cross the mountains and reach the Sacramento Valley. By this time, the horses and mules were in very poor conditions. Fremont set up camp along a tributary of the Sacramento River. This allowed the horses and mules to graze and regain their strength. The animals weren't the only ones to enjoy the rest. In the lower valley game was much more plentiful and all enjoyed a good venison steak.

Traveling down the valley, the party spotted the Coast Range of mountains. While it had been many years since Kit had been there, he still remembered the country very well. As soon as the Coast Range was spotted, he led the party straight to Sutter's Fort.

At the Fort everyone was well received, even though they were a dirty, ragged looking group of people. Here Fremont was able to get all of the supplies and equipment needed. After a few days of rest, the trip down the Sacramento valley began again. Before leaving, Fremont divided the party. Fitzpatrick was left in charge of most of the men, while Colonel Fremont chose Kit and four others to accompany him south.

Fremont traveled down the San Joaquin and across the Coast Range well south of San Francisco. The group continued south until they reached the Spanish Trail east of Los Angeles. They followed the Spanish Trail to the Mojave River. That night along the Mojave River, a Mexican man and boy came into camp. They said they were from a small party of two other men and two women. They also told Fremont they were driving a small herd of horses to the coast and were attacked by Indians. Everyone escaped, but the Indians took all of their horses. They asked Fremont if he could help getting their horses back. Fremont told the Mexican that anyone who wanted to could volunteer. Kit and one other mountain man were the only ones that wanted to help.

The Mexican man and boy stayed with Colonel Fremont while Kit and his partner left for the Mexican camp. On the way there, Kit came across the trail of the Indians. Kit and his partner changed courses and took out after the Indians. It took about two days to overtake them. The Indians had killed several of the horses and were enjoying quite a feast.

Kit and his partner were well hidden about two miles back from the Indian camp. After discussing their options, they decided to wait until evening and then try to sneak in among the horses and drive them off. Their hope was to avoid a fight with the Indians. However, this plan went like most others, it didn't work. They were able to get inside the herd unnoticed, but a young colt got excited and started raising a fuss. This alerted the Indians, who grabbed their rifles and came to see what the fuss was about. As soon as the Indians came near the herd, both men opened fire, killing two of the Indians. The rest of the Indians decided not to risk it and fled. Kit and his partner gathered the horses and started back to where Fremont was camped.

As soon as they reached Fremont, the entire party left for the Mexican camp to deliver the horses. On arrival, they found the two men dead and horribly mutilated. The two women were missing. Fremont assumed they had been captured and were being held captive by the Indians.

Fremont told Kit and four other men to find the two women and to bring them back, if at all possible. It didn't take long to find them. They had been staked to the ground, and, like the men, had been brutally mutilated. The two women were buried as rapidly as possible, and the men returned to camp. The Mexican man and boy were left with their horses, and they headed down the Spanish Trail to the California coast.

Fremont and the rest of the party took a direct route to the Arkansas River and on to Bent's Fort. They arrived at the Fort on July 2, 1844. Fremont and the rest of the men were given a big feast and celebration. This was quite a change from the diet they had become accustomed to.

Right after the Fourth of July, Fremont and Kit parted company. Fremont and the rest of his men left for the States. Kit took a direct route to Taos. Before Kit left, he looked up Fremont and said, "Colonel, it shore has been good workin' for you. Should you come back this way and want to do a little more explorin', I'd shore be proud to join you. You know where to find me if you ever need me." Kit was just turning to leave when Fremont stopped him with this comment, "Kit, I have never had a man with me that was braver or more honest than you have been. If the army ever sends me on another exploring trip, you will be the first one I will look up to join me."

On arrival at Taos Kit immediately went to see how Josefa was doing. She seemed to be doing alright and was happy to find that Kit was still alive. At first Kit had a hard time getting used to the change in diet and the quiet and solitude of a house. It took awhile before he could hear a noise at night and know it was not Indians creeping up on him.

Kit enjoyed walking around town, seeing how it had grown and talking to the few people there that he knew. On one of his walks he saw a mountain man, Dick Owens, who he had met on the Green River several years before. Kit and Dick Owens spent considerable time together. They both came to the conclusion that they had traveled enough, and it was time to settle down in one place.

During the winter, the two men decided to look for a nice tract of land along some stream and try their hand at farming. This was rather surprising given Kit's hatred for farming.

However, in the early spring the two started out and found exactly what they were looking for. This was about a two thousand acre tract located along the Little Cimarron River at Rayado, some fifty miles east of Taos. The first order of business was to build a couple of huts to show improvements. While Dick got some land ready for planting, Kit went to Santa Fe to file Homestead Papers in both of their names.

When Kit returned, they got a nice acreage of grain planted. They were in the process of cutting lumber from trees along the Little Cimarron to make improvements when two riders came into their camp. They told Kit that Colonel Fremont was at Bent's Fort and would sure like Kit to join him on another trip. Kit told the two men that he would be at Bent's Fort as soon as he possibly could.

As soon as the two men left, Kit and Owens had a short discussion and decided to sell the property, and they would both go to Bent's Fort. They put their Homestead up for sale. It didn't take long to sell the property, getting about half of what it was worth.

Kit and Owens left for Taos, where Kit had to tell Josefa that he was going on another trip with Colonel Fremont. Josefa wasn't happy with the idea but knew it would be impossible to keep Kit at home where she wished he would stay. The following morning the two men left for Bent's Fort, arriving there some three day later. On their arrival, Fremont said, "Kit, I am sure glad to see you. I can also use Owens if he is looking for work." It didn't take Dick Owens long to accept the offer.

The morning after their arrival, they started for Lake Utah. This is a fresh water lake located about 30 miles south of the Great Salt Lake. On arrival at Lake Utah they started north around the lake and up a small estuary to a point where they could see the Great Salt Lake. From this vantage point they could see another large island out in the lake. The natives told them that this island had plenty of fresh water, grass and game.

Early the next morning Fremont, Kit and two others left for the Great Salt Lake. Dick Owens was left in charge of the rest of the party. On arrival at the lake, Fremont encountered a settlement of Indians who appeared to be friendly. Using sign language, which is fairly universal among the tribes, they were told what Fremont wanted to do. They showed Fremont a canoe he could use to get across to the island. They also signed that they would care for the horses while they were gone.

They soon had their equipment transferred to the canoe and left for the island, which was about ten miles away. On arrival they did find fresh water and herds of antelope as far as the eye could see. The next couple of days were spent shooting antelope and smoke curing the meat. When sufficient meat was obtained, the canoe was loaded and the party started back to the mainland. On arrival the Indians returned the horses. Fremont gave them some cured meat to pay for the use of the canoe and for the care of the horses. After vowing eternal friendship, the horses were loaded with the cured meat and they returned to the base camp,

During Fremont's absence some trappers came by and told Owens that the land to the west could not be crossed, as there was no water and no grass for the animals. Fremont always took it as a direct challenge whenever he was told that something could not be done. His first action was to call Kit and give him the following instructions: "Kit, I want you to select two men, take whatever you need, and see if that tract of land can be crossed." Fremont also told Carson that on the evening of the second day, he would climb that small mountain just behind their camp. He would take his telescope and scan the western horizon. If Kit was able to cross and find water, he was to build a fire with lots of smoke, which would be a sign that he had accomplished his mission. Leaving Owens to assist Fremont, Kit selected two of the best Mountain men traveling with the group. Assuming short rations, they packed enough food and water to last four days.

Early the following morning, the small group started out. The land they entered was indeed a desolate area. There was absolutely no water or vegetation with the exception of an occassional greasewood bush. Their destination was a low range of hills laying about 30 miles to the west. On the afternoon of the second day they arrived at the hills and found a spring of fresh, cold water and all of the grass the animals needed.

The three men rested until evening, when Kit climbed a small hill and started a fire. As soon as the fire was going good he piled on green brush, which sent up a column of white smoke. Fremont was already scanning the horizon when he spotted the smoke. He returned to camp and informed everyone of Carson's success. Two days later Carson and his group arrived back at camp.

As soon as the combined parties crossed the desolate stretch of desert, Fremont split them up. One group, under Talbot and with Walkers as his guide, was to head for the Mary River and follow it down to the Carson River. From there, they were to follow the Carson River to the lake formed by that river. Fremont and the rest were to take a more southern route and end up at the same lake.

The Fremont group was the first to arrive. In about two days Talbot and his group came in. Again, Fremont split the group up with Talbot and his party taking the southern pass to the San Joaquin River and then on to Sutter's Fort. Fremont was going to take a more northern pass and all meet at the Fort. Again, Fremont was the first to arrive. He spent a few days purchasing supplies, which, among other things, included forty head of cattle and some horses.

After a few days rest, Fremont and his men left to see if they could find Talbot. The route taken was over a wide rocky area covered with snow. Before they could get across, the hooves of the cattle had become so sore and tender that they could no longer travel. A couple of cows were killed for meat and the rest left to fend for themselves.

Not finding Talbot, Fremont crossed the Coastal Range and headed for San Jose. On arrival, Fremont made inquiries about Talbot and heard that he was camped on the San Joaquin River.

On hearing where Talbot may be located, Fremont came to Kit and said, "Kit I want you to take a couple of men and see if you can find him. We will wait here until you return." In a few days Talbot was located, and Kit guided them back to San Jose.

As soon as the two parties were together, they started down the coast to Monterey. They were about thirty miles from their destination when Fremont received a demanding letter from General Castro of the Mexican Army. The General was demanding that Fremont and his men leave the country immediately.

Fremont was never one to back down from danger or a threat. That evening they packed their gear and retreated about ten miles to a nearby hill, where they found a partially hidden area that could be defended. It didn't take General Castro long to follow and set up his camp a short distance away. Castro had several hundred men divided among infantry, artillery and cavalry. Fremont was limited to forty men with rifles. The Fremont group was subjected to a constant barrage of cannon fire. After about three days it became evident that Castro was not going to attack, and the Fremont group was getting mighty tired of the constant noise. During the middle of the night they packed up and left for the Sacramento River.

They traveled up the Sacramento River to a small trading post, where Fremont intended to get the supplies needed for the trip home. When he arrived, some settlers came in and told him that the Indians were gathering their warriors to attack some of the small settlements in the area. They asked for his help in stopping the attacks. They also told him where the Indians were now camped. Fremont agreed to help.

Fremont left for the Indian encampment with his forty men and a few settlers who had volunteered to help. From the size of the village, it was estimated that there were approximately 1,000 braves. When Fremont and his men charged, they started shooting at anything that was still standing. This was a wholesale slaughter, with the Indians not killed fleeing in all directions. Fremont was confident that the Indians would think long and hard before trying to attack any of the settlements.

After resting for a couple of days Fremont started for the Columbia River. There was no trouble until they reached the upper end of Klamath Lake. Here he received word that the United States had declared war on Mexico.

Chapter 7
War with Mexico

The Commander of the Marine Contingent stationed at Monterey knew that Colonel Fremont was expected in a few more days. When after a week he hadn't arrived, he sent out a small scouting party to see if they could locate him. They soon learned of the trouble Fremont had had with General Castro and that Fremont had turned and was heading north. On hearing this, the Commandant sent Lieutenant Gillespie and six troopers north to overtake Fremont and bring him back to Monterey.

Gillespie and men rode hard for about 300 miles when their horses started giving out. He then had two troopers take two of the best remaining horses and continue north after

© 1962 University of Oklahoma Press

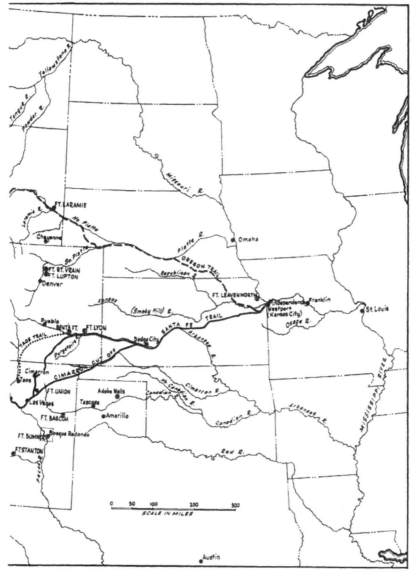

Kit Carson Country 1826-1868

Fremont. About 4 days later they found Fremont and his party at the upper end of Klamath Lake.

On hearing the news, Fremont selected ten men, including Kit Carson and Dave Owens, and started on the back trail to find Lieutenant Gillespie. The rest of the Fremont party continued north back to the States. The Fremont group traveled some sixty miles, when they came to the Gillespie camp. That night Fremont sat up until midnight reading letters from the States. Dave Owens and Kit were rolled up in saddle blankets asleep near the fire.

Shortly after midnight Fremont quit reading and lay down to sleep. A while later Kit was aroused by a noise like an axe hitting a log. Jumping up he saw that the camp was being invaded by Indians. The noise he had heard was a tomahawk crushing in the skull of one of the troopers.

Giving the alarm the camp became alert and active. Kit grabbed his pistol and shot at an Indian that had raised his tomahawk and was about to hit another member of the party. Kit's bullet hit his hand, shattering the tomahawk and completely disabling the Indian. The rest of the men started shooting, killing several Indians. The remaining Indians scattered and fled into the night. Guards were posted and the rest got what sleep they could until dawn.

The next morning looking around, it was found that three of Fremont's men had been killed, two by tomahawk and one by an arrow. The three bodies were tied to horses to take them back for proper burial.

Fremont saw Kit standing by his horse. He came over and said, "Kit, I want you to take about five men and see if there are any Indian villages close to where we are located. I feel there must be to account for that raiding party last night." Kit soon had the men he wanted and started out around the Lake. They had traveled about ten miles when they came to a fairly large Indian village of some forty lodges.

It was apparent that Kit and his group could not leave without being detected. Kit told his men that they were going to charge and do as much damage to the village as we could. They raced into the village shooting at anything that was standing. Several Indians were killed and the rest fled into the nearby hills.

They must have been fishing, as there were piles of fishing gear scattered about the lodges. There were also piles of dried fish lying about. To teach them a permanent lesson, they set fire to all of the lodges. The lodges were easy to burn as they were constructed of pine poles covered with reed mats. Fremont saw the flames and smoke and thought Kit might be in trouble. Bringing the rest of the party he came to their aid. On arrival he found that help was not needed and that the Indian problem was well under control.

When all were together again, the Fremont party left for the Sacramento Valley. They had traveled some ten miles when it became apparent that the bodies could not be transported any further. Their heads were banging against trees as they passed through a wooded area. Fremont left the trail and went inland about half of a mile, where the three bodies were buried. The burial site was covered with logs and brush so it could not be detected or disturbed.

Fremont returned to the main trail and they continued the trip south. Guards were posted every night as they were continually harassed by Indians. This continued until reaching Peter Lawson's Trading Post.

Meeting with no further difficulty, they traveled down the Sacramento River until reaching the Buttes. Here, Fremont sent two men ahead to inform the Commandant where they were located. The remainder of the group pitched camp. Since they were almost completely without supplies, a great deal of time was spent hunting for fresh meat. Fremont was also waiting for further orders as to what he was supposed to do regarding the war with Mexico.

While he was waiting, Fremont sent a small party of men to Sonoma, which he had heard had been captured by the Mexicans. When the party arrived, they had no trouble recapturing Sonoma. In the process, they took a general and two captains as prisoners. When General Castro received word of the raid, he sent a message to San Francisco, ordering a captain and a contingent of men to retake Sonoma. Meanwhile, Fremont and the rest of his group proceeded to Sonoma.

When the Mexican force drew closer, they saw the odds they were up against, and immediately turned and fled back to San Francisco. When the Mexican Army left, Fremont proceeded to Sutter's Fort, taking the prisoners with him. He commandeered the Fort for the U.S. Army. Fremont left General Vallejo and his two captains there as prisoners. He then gave a man named Lance a field commission of Commander and left him in charge of the prisoners.

As soon as problems at Sutter's Fort were under control, Fremont departed for Monterey. By this time, he had an army of approximately

150 men. The majority of the new men were American settlers who did not want to live under Mexican control. When Fremont arrived at Monterey he found that it had already been taken by the U. S. Navy under the command of Commodore Sloat. Commodore Sloat soon left, leaving Commodore Stockton in charge.

On arrival at Monterey, Fremont learned that General Castro had escaped and was now on his way to the Pueblo of Los Angeles. Knowing that Castro could not be caught by following him on land, Fremont asked for a sloop to transport him and his men to San Diego. It took about three days to make the trip south.

The troops with Fremont were either mountain men or settlers. Most had never before seen an ocean. The long ground swells off the California coast can be rather upsetting if one is not used to them. Kit was among the group feeling the greatest effect from the ocean trip. On arrival at San Diego, Kit made a promise that he would never again set foot on an ocean going vessel.

On arrival at San Diego, Fremont set small groups of men out over the countryside to collect as many horses as they could find. Needless to say, if they found any horses belonging to Mexicans those horses were obtained rather cheaply. If the horses were owned by American settlers, they were offered a fair price, which would be paid by the United States Government.

As soon as Fremont had a sufficient number of horses, he and his men started for Los Angeles. On arrival outside of Los Angeles, Fremont and his group set up camp. He was waiting for the arrival of Commodore Stockton, who he knew wanted to be present when they made their attack on Los Angeles. In a short time Commodore Stockton arrived, and the push on Los Angeles began. When they entered the Pueblo of Los Angeles they found that General Castro had fled to Sonoma, and the rest of the Mexican Army had fled to wherever they felt they might be safe. It is rather interesting to note that General Castro had an army of 700 men while Colonel Fremont and Commodore Stockton had a combined force of about 150 men.

As soon as the Pueblo of Los Angeles was secure, Colonel Fremont and Commodore Stockton retired for a private meeting. When the meeting was over Fremont summoned Kit. When Kit arrived Fremont said, "Kit, the Commodore and I have a packet of letters we want delivered to the military headquarters in Washington. Pick about fifteen good men to go

Commodore Robert F. Stockton, U.S. Navy

with you. You are to leave immediately after they have been selected."

Kit had been given sixty days in which to get to Washington. The trip proceeded without problems until they were about 20 miles from the copper mines on the Gila River. At that point, an Apache village was spotted. After a short discussion, they came to the conclusion that it would be impossible to get around the village without being spotted. It was decided that the best procedure would be to approach the village as close as possible and then make their presence known. Kit and his group were able to get about 100 yards from the village before they were seen. The Apaches were at first startled and then made rapid preparations to defend their village. Kit, who had some knowledge of the Apache language, stepped forward and told them that they had come as friends. He further told them that they were on their way to New Mexico to trade for some new horses. The Apaches, never one to pass up a good deal, informed Kit that since they had come as friends that they could stay there and do their horse trading. Most of the horses in Kit's group were pretty well run down, so this was a welcome offer. In a few days all of the men had new and better horses and were again on their way to Washington.

Around the first of October 1843, Kit's group encountered General Kearny and his military contingent. Kearny ordered Kit to join his army and guide them to their destination in California. With those orders Kit turned the packet of letters over to Fitzpatrick, who he had chosen to go with him. He also gave Fitzpatrick complete instructions as to where the letters were to go. With this accomplished, Kit turned and started back to California. General Kearny told him that their destination was San Diego, to help bolster the troops that were already there.

The route taken to California was well known to Kit. They traveled across the desert with very few problems. About the first of December 1846, they reached Warren's ranch, and here they rested for a day before continuing the trip to San Diego.

Shortly after leaving Warren's ranch, a Mexican carrying dispatches back to Mexican Headquarters in Santa Fe was captured. From these dispatches it was learned that American Forces had been run out of Monterey and Santa Barbara. The Mexican Army had also retaken Los Angeles. According to the dispatches, all American troops were now gathered in San Diego. With this knowledge, a direct course for San Diego was set.

General Stephen W. Kearny, U.S. Army

About a week later General Kearny received word that a contingent of about 100 Mexican troops were stationed on the route Kit had selected. The General sent a Lieutenant Hammond with a few troops ahead to investigate the Mexican camp. They had just come in sight of their camp, which was located in the center of an Indian village, when they were spotted by a Mexican guard. Lieutenant Hammond and his troops immediately retreated back to General Kearny.

When the General got the information that Lieutenant Hammond had gathered, he held a short meeting with his Senior Officers in which Kit was included. The decision was made to attack the Mexican camp. Early the next morning, the American troops packed their gear and started forward. Kit was in the lead group. When they were about a mile from the Mexican camp, they ran into some guards that had been posted on the trail. The Americans gave chase, but the Mexicans reached their camp before they could be caught.

When the Americans reached the Mexican camp the battle was on. This battle lasted for maybe fifteen minutes when the Mexican Army decided it would be wise to retreat. The General ordered Kit to go with Captain Johnston and his group in pursuit. They had traveled about a mile when Kit's horse stumbled and fell. His horse scrambled to its feet and took off into the brush. When Kit hit the ground, his rifle broke in several places and was now useless. Since he was in the lead group, he had to scramble out of the way to keep from being run over. There he was without a horse or rifle.

Kit started walking and, before long, spotted a dead dragoon slumped over his horse. Since he no longer had any worldly needs, Kit took his rifle, bullet pouch, and horse. He soon caught up and rejoined the battle. This battle lasted about two days with the advantage going back and forth.

On the evening of the second day, General Kearny held a conference and asked for any volunteers who thought they could get by the Mexican lines. He wanted a message delivered to San Diego asking for assistance from the U.S. Military. Kit spoke up and said, "General I ain't seen a Mexican yet I couldn't get around. I will take any letter you want delivered and have it there by tomorrow night." No sooner had Kit volunteered when Lieutenant Beale said he would also go. The General told the two men to come back in an hour when it was dark, and he would have the message ready.

An hour later, Lieutenant Beale and Kit arrived at the General's tent. When they arrived, the General said, "Lieutenant, here is the message I want delivered to the Commandant at the San Diego Military Headquarters. Kit, I want you to take the lead in getting past the Mexicans and finding the shortest route to San Diego. Good luck and God's speed to both of you."

About an hour later when it was completely dark and before the moon had come up, Beale and Kit set out. When they were about 100 yards from the Mexican line, Kit whispered to Beale, "Take off your boots and we will crawl on hands and knees to be as quiet as possible. Tie your boots to your belt and don't let them bounce on the ground."

They hadn't crawled very far when Kit glanced to his right and saw a Mexican sentry leaning on his rifle. Just at that moment Beale hit a small stone that bounced down the hill. Both men froze where they were. The sentry stared in the direction of the sound. A short time later he returned to his relaxed position. He must have come to the conclusion that it was a small animal scurrying through the brush that caused the sound. As soon as the sentry relaxed, Kit and Lieutenant Beale continued their forward progress.

It took about two hours for the two men to get past the Mexican lines. When they were finally able to stand, they found they had another problem. Both men had lost their boots and would have to continue their journey barefooted. This meant walking over small stones and prickly pears for the rest of the trip.

On the evening of the next day, the two reached San Diego. By this time, the Lieutenant was almost gone mentally and physically and was essentially carried by Kit for the last few miles. On reaching the military post, Kit asked to see the Commandant. After explaining the reason for the meeting, they were taken to the Commandant's tent and shown in. Much to Kit's surprise, the man in charge was Commodore Stockton. His first words were, "Kit, what are you doing here? You're supposed to be in Washington." Kit explained to the Commodore what had happened and why he was there. He then handed Stockton the letter which he had earlier taken from the Lieutenant's uniform pocket.

As soon as the letter was read, Stockton called his aide and gave him orders to assemble an army and go to the assistance of General Kearny. While this was in progress, Kit drew a detailed map showing the location of the Mexican

Army and the camp of General Kearny. By two o'clock in the morning, the U.S. Army was ready to leave.

Kit stayed behind in San Diego for some much needed rest. Lieutenant Beale was taken aboard ship to sick bay for a long recuperation By the next day, Kit felt ready to go again (Particularly after being issued a pair of new boots).

On leaving San Diego, the U.S. Army made a forced march to the Mexican line. When the Mexican Army saw them approach, they decided it would be wise to retreat. This they did in a non-military fashion. They scattered and ran in all directions. As soon as the Mexican Army had departed, the U.S. contingent proceeded on to General Kearny's camp. The General's first question when they arrived was about the condition of Kit and Lieutenant Beale. He wasn't too surprised when he got the report of their condition as best as the leader of the U.S. troops knew it. After a short rest for the San Diego troops, General Kearny broke camp and followed them back to San Diego.

The General stayed in San Diego for about a month to give his troops time to rest and recover from the wounds they had received. When everyone had recovered, General Kearny and Commodore Stockton started for Los Angeles with a combined force of approximately 600 men. When they were about 15 miles from the Pueblo of Los Angeles, they found that the Mexican Army had occupied a small hill situated right in their path.

After discussing the situation, it was decided to turn the next move over to Commodore Stockton. He set up two cannons that he had brought along. When a volley was fired, the Mexicans watched the cannon balls hit. They rapidly decided that this was not the type of life they desired and retreated back to the Pueblo of Los Angeles. It took about two days for the American Forces to capture the Pueblo of Los Angeles. The Americans took control of the Pueblo the first part of January 1847.

On leaving Los Angeles, the Mexican Army headed north to engage Colonel Fremont, who they had heard was on his way to Los Angeles. The one thing that they hadn't heard was that Fremont now had an army of approximately 400 men. These were primarily volunteers he had picked up from settlements along the way. When the two armies met, the Mexican Army decided to surrender rather than flee. Colonel Fremont was about the only officer the Mexicans were willing to trust. As soon as the Colonel, his men, and his prisoners arrived in Los Angeles, Kit left General Kearny and returned to Colonel Fremont.

When all of the troops were settled and in their proper station, General Kearny, Commodore Stockton, and Colonel Fremont retired to the General's tent for a lengthy discussion. During this meeting, letters were prepared for both the Departments of the Army and Navy in Washington. These letters were to bring the two Departments up-to-date on conditions in California. The letters also requested orders for future campaigns for the California Military.

While California was warm and sunny, the rest of the country was experiencing a harsh winter. Travel across country would be almost impossible. The first part of March an adjutant was sent out to bring both Kit and Lieutenant Beale to the General's tent. Why Lieutenant Beale had been called was a mystery to Kit. He had recovered enough to make the trip to Los Angeles, but was in no condition to make the long trip east to Washington. However, Kit was learning that orders from Washington didn't always make sense.

On arrival at the General's tent, Kit was given letters for the Department of the Army, and Lieutenant Beale was given letters for the Navy Department.

The following morning, the Lieutenant and Kit started out for Washington. Kit's suspicions about the Lieutenant's health were confirmed. For the first twenty or so days, Kit had to help him in and out of his saddle. Kit was particularly alert for any signs of trouble as he knew the Lieutenant would be of no help in any type of conflict. Luckily, no trouble was encountered.

On their way to Washington, they passed through St. Louis. While there, Kit had the honor of meeting Colonel Benton, who offered him his home in Washington as a place to stay during his time there. This was an offer Kit readily accepted. The Lieutenant and Kit stayed two days in St. Louis then left again on their trip east. They arrived in Washington in June 1847.

One of the first people Kit met in Washington was Lieutenant Beale's mother. She must have been satisfied with the care Kit had shown her son as she showered every kindness on him. Lieutenant Beale had now recovered enough to conduct his own business. The first thing they both did was to deliver the letters to the proper authorities.

After a visit with the Department of the Army, Kit had free time to visit old friends and to see the new sights that had been developed around Washington since his last visit. The latter part of June, he was summoned to the White House for a meeting with President Polk. President Polk wanted a first hand evaluation of conditions in California. He also had a particular concern about a rumor he had heard of a conflict between Commodore Stockton and General Kearny. Kit told the President, quite honestly, that he thought Commodore Stockton was the better man, but that he knew of no conflict. President Polk then took Kit completely by surprise by giving him a Commission as Lieutenant of Rifles. When this was completed, Kit was handed a packet of letters to be delivered to California as soon as possible. He soon learned that Lieutenant Beale had been given a similar packet for the Navy. The two men started for California the following day.

They had gotten as far as St. Louis when the Lieutenant again completely gave out. Kit took his packet of letters and assured him that they would be delivered to the proper people. The Lieutenant was to return to Washington after he had recovered enough to make the trip. After seeing that the Lieutenant was being tended too, Kit continued his trip west.

James K. Polk
President of the United States 1845-1849

On reaching Fort Leavenworth, Kit was informed that the Comanche Indians were on the warpath. He was assigned 50 men to accompany him for the rest of the trip. There was no trouble until they reached Pawnee Rock. Here they met a large company of volunteers, a herd of cattle, and a wagon train all heading for New Mexico. When they set up camp for the night, the two parties were about a quarter of a mile apart.

The next morning while the New Mexico party was moving their horses to greener fields, they were attacked by the Comanches. It appeared that their only objective was to run off the horses and cattle. However, the cattle didn't cooperate when they turned directly toward Kit's camp. The horses must have thought this was a good idea as they turned and followed the cattle. The Comanches departed when one of their braves was killed by rifle fire. Kit returned the horses and cattle to the New Mexico group. The next morning Kit and his men continued on to Santa Fe.

On arrival at Santa Fe, Kit dismissed the group of men he had been given at Fort Leavenworth. After they were dismissed, he picked up sixteen men of his own choosing. There was minimal trouble the rest of the way and they arrived in Los Angeles during October 1847.

On arrival in Los Angeles, Kit found that the Command Center had been moved to Monterey. He immediately departed for that location. On arrival he delivered the Washington messages to Colonel Mason, the officer in charge.

Kit was only in Monterey on a few days when he was ordered back to Los Angeles. On arrival he was assigned some 30 dragoons under the command of Captain Smith. Their duty was to guard the area against any Indian depredation. This was primarily guarding the Tejon Pass. This was essentially the only pass through the San Gabriel Mountains. The Indians used this pass to move stolen horses and cattle out of the Los Angeles basin. This duty lasted until spring, when Kit was again ordered to take a packet of letters back to Washington.

In the spring of 1848, Kit left with a party of sixteen volunteers for Washington. Knowing that the men he had with him were inexperienced in fighting Indians, he did his best to avoid any confrontations. The small parties they did meet were no trouble. This was particularly true when they found that Kit could talk to them in their native tongue.

About the middle of April they arrived in Taos. That night he brought Josefa up to date on what had been happening. The next morning he left the men in Taos and went to Santa Fe. At Santa Fe he met with Colonel Newby of the Illinois Volunteers, who brought him up to date on Indian problems he might run into. He was also told that the Comanches were still on the warpath and should be avoided if at all possible.

Kit returned to Taos and selected ten of the best men in his party to accompany him the rest of the way to Washington. Kit and his men stayed in Taos for several days to give the men time to get the equipment they would need. Kit spent his time taking care of Josefa's needs.

When Kit arrived back from Santa Fe, he was wearing the uniform of a Lieutenant. Since he had failed to tell Josefa about the commission when he first arrived, this took her completely by surprise. Her first question was, "Kit, when did you become an officer in the U.S. Army?" When he told her what had happened in Washington, she seemed quite pleased.

When the men had the equipment they needed, Kit started for Washington. He had packed his uniform for use in Washington and was again in his frontier garb. Josefa was unhappy that he had to leave so soon.

Christopher "Kit" Carson

Being aware of the Comanche problems they traveled well north of their normal range. They reached Fort Leavenworth without seeing any Indians.

On reaching Fort Leavenworth, Kit was informed that his commission had not been approved by the Senate and was therefore invalid. On hearing the news, his men thought it best to leave the letters with the Fort Commander and return west. After giving the matter serious thought, Kit concluded that it made little difference whether he was considered an Army officer or an experienced mountain man. He was probably proudest of the fact that he was considered the best man to carry the letters to Washington.

On reaching Washington Kit delivered the letters entrusted to him. He also learned that a treaty had been signed with Mexico. The war was now officially over. He felt vindicated for his decision, as he would have lost his commission at that time regardless of what he did.

Chapter 8
Post War Activities

As soon as the letters were delivered, Kit left Washington and headed for Taos by way of St. Louis. After a few days visit in St. Louis he continued his trip to Taos, arriving there in October 1848.

Kit stayed in Taos that fall and winter, which for him was a long stay in any one place. However, he did make several short trips with Colonel Beall, who had the responsibility for keeping Indians on their reservation. This appeared to be a never-ending job.

The biggest problem was found in one of the conditions inserted into the Mexican Treaty. This condition stated that the U.S. Government would return to Mexico all Mexican prisoners held by the Indians. The Indians felt they had given up enough without having to give up their Mexican slaves.

Prior to one of the above-mentioned trips, the Colonel got word of a large Indian encampment on the Republican River. The Colonel sent word asking Kit to join him as a guide. While it was never mentioned, he was also used as an interpreter, since he could talk to the various tribes in their native tongue.

When they arrived at the Indian encampment they found it to be larger than expected. It was estimated that there were about 2,000 people there. Colonel Beall asked for a parley with their chiefs. When the parley started he requested that Kit act as interpreter. The first thing the Colonel wanted was the return of all Mexican prisoners. The Indians, seeing that the army was greatly outnumbered, refused to comply. The Colonel knew that they could not force them, so he decided the best course of action would be to retreat and wait for a future treaty to be negotiated with that tribe.

While Kit was in Taos he met a Mr. Maxwell. During his visits with him they made plans for a settlement on a tributary of the Republican River. They felt that this would be a very profitable venture. It was also a place where they could spend more time with their wives and children. This plan didn't last very long due to the Apache Indians. They were continually raiding settlements and homesteads throughout the area. In addition, they were murdering any people who might have been traveling through the area. Because of this, Kit was constantly being called on as a guide and interpreter.

While Kit never had any fear about going into an Indian fight, it must have caused Josefa a great deal of anxiety. She never knew if she was going to see him alive again. It is amazing that she never let Kit see her fears. Her only comment when he left was always wishing he could spend more time at home.

On one of these missions, they were after a party of Indians that had ambushed a small group heading for New Mexico. All of the men had been slain. A Mrs. White, the wife of one of the slain men, had been taken prisoner. Kit and his company found the place where the ambush had occurred and buried the bodies as rapidly as possible.

They found the trail of the Indians and started following it as fast as they could. At each camp the Indians would split up into small groups of two or three and take off in all directions. By evening they would all meet at some predetermined spot. It didn't take long to figure out what they were doing. This made the job of following them much easier. At each camp they found one or two items of clothing belonging to Mrs. White. This renewed their hope that she was still alive.

Some ten days later they finally came in sight of the Indian camp. They were completely unaware of the army's presence. Kit started to charge their camp calling for the men to follow him. However, the Commander in charge called a halt, hoping to set up a parley. As soon as the Indians became aware of the army's presence, they started moving out, many running naked through the brush. On entering the camp Kit found Mrs. White with an arrow through her heart. Had they continued the initial charge, Kit was sure they would have saved her. However, the treatment she had endured was so brutal that she could not have lived very long.

After the battle, the army left for Barclay's fort on the Mora River. They had barely started when they were hit by the worst storm Kit had ever seen. Because of the storm, they lost all sense of direction. Luckily, They ran into some thick timber that offered some protection from the storm. One of the men froze to death. Later it was learned that many of the Indians they had been tracking had also perished in the storm.

As soon as the storm cleared up, Kit was able to get his bearings. At this point the Commander decided to bypass Barclay's Fort and head directly for Taos. Kit was in Taos only a short time when he decided to leave for Rayado where there was a small military detachment. He was there until the spring of 1850.

Kit had only one problem while he was there. Their reserve herd of horses had been moved to a pasture a little over a mile from where they were camped. The herd was watched by two of the soldiers. During the night, a small group of Indians drove off the horses and severely wounded the two guards. One of the guards was able to come back to camp and sound the alarm. As normal practice the riding stock was kept close to camp, without waste of time the men were able to saddle up and give chase.

The Indians were traveling fast and, by that evening, must have felt they had gotten away. When Kit came in sight of their camp, the Indians were laying around a small fire completely relaxed. Kit and his group charged their camp killing five Indians. The remaining three or four made their escape into the brush.

Kit and his men were able to round up all but two or three of their horses. When they had the horses settled down, they started back to Rayado. Shortly after returning, Kit left for Taos.

Kit was only in Taos a few days when he received a message from Tim Goodel. Tim was a well-known rancher in that area and was asking for Kit's help. He wanted to take a herd of horses and mules to Fort Laramie to trade with the immigrants. The first part of May 1850 they started out with a herd of about 50 animals. It took a little over a month to reach Fort Laramie and another month to dispose of all of the animals. They bargained with the immigrants and made a very nice profit. As previously agreed, Goodel split the profit with Kit.

When all trades were complete, Goodel left for California and Kit returned to Taos. Kit traveled without problems until he reached the Arkansas River. There at a small settlement, he was told that the Apaches were on the warpath and murdering any travelers that came by.

Kit stayed at the settlement for about six days gathering a small herd of horses he wanted to take back to Taos. Kit also wanted to get some men to go with him to help, in case of trouble. However, all he could recruit was a young Mexican boy and an older settler to go with him.

Kit and his two helpers left the settlement late in the afternoon and started for Taos. They took a route about a mile off the main trail and held to this route until the following morning. At first daylight, the horses were hidden in the brush to graze and rest. While the two helpers took turns sleeping and watching the stock, Kit climbed the highest cottonwood tree he could find up to where he had a good view of the main trail which was now a little less than a mile away. His only problem was trying to stay awake. He stayed in that tree all day watching for Indians. Toward evening he saw a large group of Indians on the trail going in the opposite direction they were headed. When they were well past, Kit climbed down. They saddled up, gathered the stock, and started out. For the next 15 or 20 miles they stayed off the main trail. They now returned to the trail and had no further problems the rest of the way into Taos.

At Taos, Kit settled in for an extended stay. However, it wasn't long before he received a message from Rayado, reporting that they had encountered trouble and needed his help. When Josefa heard about the trouble, the first thing she said was, "Kit, when is the world going to leave you alone, and you can stay home for more than a few days?" Kit told her that he hadn't asked for this, but neither would he ignore their request for help.

Lieutenant Taylor of the First Dragoons was stationed in Taos. Kit went to him and told him about his mission. He assigned ten dragoons to accompany him. They left the following morning for Rayado. On arrival, they found that the Indian problem had been resolved. The ten dragoons were released to return to Taos. Instead of returning with the dragoons, Kit stayed at Rayado until March 1851.

A Mr. Maxwell came to Rayado looking for an escort to take 12 wagons to St. Louis for supplies. Since Kit hadn't been to St. Louis for quite awhile, he volunteered to go. Kit was also assigned a small detachment of dragoons to accompany the wagon train. It took about two weeks to reach St. Louis. On arrival they purchased the requested supplies. Kit took a few days to visit friends before starting back.

The return trip went smooth until about 15 miles from the Arkansas River. Here they ran into a party of Cheyenne Indians. Kit greeted them and then went on for another ten miles before making camp.

As soon as they stopped, he sent the dragoons on ahead to Rayado to bring back a larger escort. While the Cheyenne Indians appeared friendly, there was something about their behavior that told Kit to be cautious. His biggest worry was that he was now left with two volunteers and 13 Mexicans. He had very little faith in the Mexicans' bravery. That evening, Cheyenne Warriors started coming into camp. They came in small groups of two or three at a time. Kit asked them to sit and smoke. This they did until there was about 20 warriors in camp. At this point they started talking among themselves. They were completely unaware that Kit could understand their language. He understood them to say they could kill him with a knife while he was distracted smoking. As for the Mexicans, they could be killed like so many buffalo. At this point Kit told them that they would have to leave and that he would shoot anyone who didn't go. He also told them that he had sent the dragoons on ahead to bring back reinforcements. The Indians sent a small party out to the trail to check his story. When they saw that what Kit had said was true, they returned and left for their camp.

The wagon train traveled on to Rayado without further incident. On their arrival, they learned the reason for the Cheyenne animosity. Apparently, a U.S. Army officer had flogged a Cheyenne chief for some misdeed. No Indian would take this kind of insult without some type of revenge. It didn't matter who received the revenge as long as it was a person of the same race. As it happened, Kit was the first white man they had seen since the flogging. Therefore, Kit was the one chosen for revenge. After Kit delivered the supplies, Mr. Maxwell pulled him aside and presented a proposal. He had heard that beaver were again becoming plentiful. Maxwell would supply the men and equipment if Kit would take charge of a trapping party for that winter. On return, they would split any profits that were made. As soon as all preparations were complete, Kit started out with a party of 18 men. They took a direct route to New Park where they started trapping the streams in that area. When that area was covered, they proceeded on to the Laramie River. Here they trapped the main river and all of the tributaries along it. By that spring they had a good load of beaver pelts. They packed up and started back to Rayado, arriving there during August 1853.

After the pelts were sold and the profits divided, Mr. Maxwell asked Kit if he would be interested in another venture. He told Kit that mutton was in great demand by the California gold miners around Sacramento. Kit told Mr. Maxwell that he was very interested. Kit immediately started south to some of the larger sheep ranches where he purchased over six thousand head of sheep. When the purchases were complete, he started back to Rayado. On arrival he found that Mr. Maxwell had hired some herders to assist him on the trip to California.

As soon as trails were open they left for Fort Laramie. From there they took the emigrant road to California, arriving there during the summer of 1854. It didn't take long to dispose of the sheep at a good profit. While finalizing the sale, Kit received a message from Mr. Maxwell telling him that he was in Los Angeles. He wanted Kit to meet him there so they could travel back to New Mexico together. Kit arrived back in Taos during late December 1854.

When he arrived home, Josefa met him at the door. Before she even greeted him, she said, "Kit, you have been appointed Indian Agent for this area."

Chapter 9
Indian Agent

On receiving word of his appointment, Kit went directly to Army Headquarters in Taos and paid the required bond for the job.

Shortly after paying the bond, he left for Santa Fe to take care of some of the required business for the Indian Agent position. About the same time he was in Santa Fe, the Jicartilla Apaches became quite hostile and showed signs of war. They came within 20 miles of Taos. At this point the Army sent out troops under the command of Lieutenant Beall.

When the troops came in contact with the Apaches, they found them well hidden behind trees, rocks and brush. Two troopers were killed and an unknown number of Indians were shot. On Kit's return from Santa Fe, he came across the battlefield. He found no signs of Indians anywhere in the area.

Shortly after his return from Santa Fe, the Apaches again approached Taos. As before, the Army sent out troops to drive then back to their reservation. This time the Apaches appeared ready to do battle. They had picked a mountain with plenty of trees and brush for them to hide. As soon as the troops arrived, the battle was on. The troops could not see the Indians, who were well hidden by the trees and brush.

Since the mountain was too steep and covered with too much brush the troopers could not use their horses. Because of these problems the Army set up a camp along a stream at the base of the mountain. As soon as the camp was established, the Army charged the Indians on foot. Whenever an Apache was dislodged he merely went back up hill and joined the rest of his people.

The battle lasted all day, and by evening the Army had to retreat. The Army had lost 22 troopers with many more wounded. The number of Indians killed was unknown.

When the troopers carrying their dead arrived back in Taos, the Officer in Charge, a Lieutenant Colonel Cooke, immediately assembled his troops and started after the

Apaches to teach them a lesson. However, prior to leaving, he came and asked Kit to join him as chief tracker and interpreter. Since it was his job to see that the Indians behaved and stayed on their reservation, Kit could not refuse.

The trail of the Apaches was picked up about 15 miles southwest of Taos. The Apaches were traveling at a leisurely pace and crossing some of the roughest terrain Kit had ever seen. The land was crisscrossed with deep ravines and streams at their flood stage. These streams had to be crossed and trails found down and up out of the ravines. At the start of the chase the Apaches were traveling as a group. They must have spotted the troops because they reverted to their old ways. At each camp they would break up into small groups and take off in all directions. This time, however, there was one major difference. If the wrong group was chosen to follow, the troops could end up right back where they started. It didn't take long to give up this tracking procedure and head directly for their homeland. Three days later the troops came to an Apache village. As soon as it was spotted the army charged. During the attack they killed about seven Apaches. When the battle started, the Apaches scattered and ran into the brush. The soldiers followed killing several more

Indians. That night on returning to the Indian village the troops set up camp. The next morning the wounded men were sent back to Taos for medical attention. They were accompanied by a Corporal and a small squad of troopers.

On the way back to Taos with the wounded men they encountered a lone Indian. The troopers immediately took him prisoner and confiscated his horse and equipment. The Indian, a member of the Utah tribe, escaped and returned to his people.

When the troops and Kit returned to Taos they were told of the incident. This caused a great deal of concern. The Utah Indians had always been friendly and Kit didn't want them to go on the warpath. When Kit heard what had happened, he sent a man to the Utah village to tell the chiefs he wanted to talk to them. In a few days the Utah chiefs arrived at the Agency Office to vent their displeasure. They told Kit that the Utah had always tried to be friends and asked why the white men had acted as they did. Kit told them how sorry he was and that the troopers thought the man they had captured was an Apache. Kit made sure that the horse and equipment were returned. In addition, each chief was given a blanket as a token of friendship. With that, they promised to remain friends. When they left the Agency Office and started back to their village, they all agreed that it was only a stupid white man that couldn't tell the difference between a Utah and an Apache Indian.

Shortly after Lieutenant Colonel Cooke returned back to Taos, Major Carlton made preparations for a campaign against the Apaches. Again, Kit was asked to accompany him as chief scout and interpreter. They left Taos and headed north. On the second day they turned south to the White Mountains and followed this range to the Sangre de Cristo range. They followed the Sangre de Cristo Mountains to the Sangre de Cristo Pass on their way to the Mosco Pass. Kit started picking up Apache signs and knew they were on the right course.

At the entrance to Mosco Pass they found an old Apache village. As before, the trail led through very rough country of ravines, valleys and rivers. On the sixth day Kit and his company overtook the Apaches. As soon as the Apaches were spotted, Major Carlton and his troops charged. The Apaches were taken completely by surprise. During the initial attack, three Apaches were killed. The rest scattered and ran into the thick brush surrounding their encampment. As a result of this engagement the troops were able to capture about 40 head of their horses.

They tried to locate the Apaches in the brush, but it was too thick. As soon as the futility of the search became apparent, the engagement stopped. The troops were assembled and the return trip to Taos was started. A small contingent of troopers, under the command of Captain Quinn, remained at the village in case any of the Indians should return. Luckily, one of the Indian trackers remaining with Captain Quinn knew the rallying call of the Apaches. In a short time two men and two women came into camp. The troopers fired, killing one of the men. The shooting and noise of the engagement alerted the rest of the Apaches that the army was nearby. No other Apaches returned to their village. With that, Captain Quinn ordered his men to retreat. They soon rejoined Major Carlton. They arrived back in Taos in June of that year.

On arrival in Taos, Kit's first stop was to let Josefa know he was home and still alive. He then went to his Headquarters, where he received a most unpleasant surprise. The Chief Clerk informed Kit that Washington was waiting for his reports. He still hadn't learned to read or write. He had always been told everything he needed to know. Learning to read and write would not improve his ability to track a man or animal so he never saw the need.

Since Kit had never made out a report in his life, he asked the Chief Clerk for his assistance. Kit's first question was, "what does Washington want to know"? He was told "everything". This sure didn't simplify the task. Kit asked the Clerk to give him a hand as he sure didn't know how to make one out. The hardest part was what Washington called a financial statement. They wanted to know the monies that had been spent for purchases during his duties as Indian Agent. Kit had no idea how to set a price on a bartered item. When you trade a bag of coffee for a bag of shot and powder, how do you get a cost? Here you are receiving an item with the same value as the item given. Kit told the Clerk to write down whatever he thought would keep Washington happy. It took some three days to get the report written and ready to send to Washington. In his experience Kit had found that it was much easier to fight Indians than it was to make out reports.

Kit did not engage in any other Indian activities until fall. At that time he made a trip to the Utah village to invite the chiefs to Albuquerque for a meeting with the Superintendent of Indian Affairs. The Utah village was about 200 miles from Taos. On the way there, Kit had to skirt an Apache village. He was able to pass their village without being detected and arrived at the Utah village without incident. After receiving assurance that they would attend the meeting, Kit returned to Taos.

One of his duties as Indian Agent was to attend such meetings. The first of October Kit left Taos for Albuquerque. He arrived there two days before the Utah chiefs. When the chiefs arrived, they were dressed in their finest ceremonial attire. Their tunics and breeches were covered in intricate designs formed with beads, porcupine quills and rattlesnake rattles. Kit had to learn not to jump every time they moved as it sounded like a room full of rattlesnakes.

The first thing the chiefs wanted to discuss was the murder of one of their braves. They told the Superintendent that the brave had been shot by some Mexicans who wanted to steal his coat. They wanted to be given some horses as payment for his death. They also wanted the Mexicans captured and brought to justice. The request for horses was denied, but they were promised that the Mexicans would be captured and brought to justice. After much discussion and debate the chiefs said that they were satisfied with the outcome of the meeting.

The Utah chiefs finally agreed to remain friends and do no harm to the white settlers in the area. When assurances of friendship were received, each chief was given a robe and sent on his way.

Not too long after the council ended, one of the chiefs came down with smallpox. In fairly rapid succession, the rest of the chiefs became ill with the disease. The Utah people were convinced that the white people, and in particular the Superintendent of Indian Affairs, had deliberately brought the smallpox to them. With that, the Utah Nation decided to join the Apaches and attack any white people they might find. It wasn't long before the entire Southwest was under siege.

When the Indian uprising began, the Governor of New Mexico appointed Captain St. Vrain with the responsibility of bringing the Indians under control. Kit had known the Captain for many years and felt he was an ideal selection for this job. In fact it was one of the few decisions the Governor had made that met with complete approval of the people.

During the early winter of 1855, Colonel Fauntleroy arrived in Taos with a large contingent of men. He immediately decided to wage a campaign against the Apache Indians and all other tribes that had joined them. The troops left Taos with four companies of men under the command of the newly appointed Colonel St. Vrain and headed for the Apache homeland. Kit went along with the Army as principal guide and interpreter. In approximately ten days they came to a large Indian settlement which was immediately attacked. During this attack many of the braves were killed before they could scatter and hide in the surrounding brush. The troops gathered up all of the horses they could find and then destroyed all of the standing property.

After the battle a small group of men were left at the Indian camp in the event any should return. The rest of the Command, Kit included, went in pursuit of the fleeing Indians. In about a week the Apaches were finally overtaken at the headwaters of the Arkansas River. When the Indians were spotted, the troops charged with the same results as in the first battle. After the battle, Colonel Fauntleroy felt the Indians had been chastised enough and preparations were made to return to Taos.

When the Superintendent of Indian Affairs heard of the Army's success he immediately sent word for all tribes to come to Albuquerque to sign a peace treaty. Most of the tribes that were present did sign, while a few refused to do so.

After the signing ceremony the Superintendent doled out gifts to the various chiefs. These gifts could be a blanket, some colored cloth, beads, paint or a small packet of sugar. One Utah chief received an old ragged blanket, which he immediately tore up and vowed to kill the Superintendent. He was lucky in that he was restrained by his people and was not permitted to carry out his threat.

Kit looked at these gifts with dismay. Any Indian could earn more in furs from one day's hunting than he was receiving from the Superintendent. However, as usual, the Government felt they were being quite generous. When all of the Indians had left for their homeland, the Superintendent left for Washington with the treaties for ratification by the Congress. It seems that Congress felt they had more important business, as the treaties were never ratified.

On returning to Taos, Kit found that Colonel St. Vrain was preparing for another foray against the Indians who had not signed the peace treaty. Kit told the Colonel that he could not join him as he had too much to do at home as Indian Agent. Kit went to the Agency Office daily, and hardly a day passed that he didn't receive a group of Indians with some kind of complaint. It was a common feeling among all tribes that he should be able to settle all complaints without seeking Government permission.

During this period of time the only person that was really happy was Josefa. She was thankful that Kit was staying home most of the time. She tried to please him by cooking special dinners that she felt he would enjoy. However, the meals were so foreign to what he had become used to that his stomach started to rebel. When it got too bad, Kit would take a short trip to some Indian village to let his system settle. As time went on, he found that he could stay in Taos for longer and longer periods of time.

While this might seem to have been calmer period of time there were still many problems to be resolved. As mentioned earlier, the Utah Indians had joined with the Apaches and were raiding white settlers throughout the area. Solving these problems was not in line with an Indian Agents duties. This was usually a matter the army would have to settle.

Even though the Utah and Apache Indians were allied, the Utah Indians were not above stealing horses from the Apaches. In general, Kit could negotiate a return of the horses. It soon became apparent that stealing horses was more of a game than any need for horses.

During April 1857, Kit had his final report prepared as Indian Agent. His term as Indian Agent would be over at the end of the month. Kit thought that he could now do some of the things he had always wanted to do. However, this was a short-lived period of his life. In May of that year he was asked to be Indian Agent again for the same three tribes, the Navajo, the Apache, and the Utah Indians, or Utes as they were now called. The last of May Kit posted the necessary bond and was sworn in as Indian Agent for the three tribes.

One of the first problems Kit encountered was with the Tabiguache Utes. They were the largest segment of the Ute Tribe, but were not assigned to any Indian Agency. When Kit reported this fact to Washington, the Government in all its wisdom said fine, they are now your responsibility.

On getting this added responsibility, Kit encountered one major problem. During the spring and summer of 1858, the Mormons were pouring into the Great Salt Lake Basin. The Mormons were trying to ally themselves with the Utes to keep General Albert S. Johnston out of the Salt Lake Basin. Kit was finally able to break up the alliance by offering the Utes an increased food allowance.

Even without the Utes, the Mormons were at war with the United States in their attempt to set up a sovereign nation in Utah. This was in fact a bloodless war, but it did cause a great deal of concern. In addition to the Mormons, the Navajos were trying to negotiate a peace with the Utes. While this appeared friendly, it was not known what would take place once the two tribes came together. The problem expanded when the Utes and Navajos included the Cheyennes in their peace parley.

The peace parley came to a rapid end when the Utes complained to Kit that the Navajos were persecuting their people. The peace treaty was also disrupted when the Utes killed some Navajo and Cheyenne warriors.

The Navajo people were without a doubt the richest tribe in the Southwest. They had large fields of grain, squash, and melons. They also had large herds of horses, mules, and sheep. Their weaving techniques were highly developed, so they were never without clothes or blankets. In spite of these assets, they were prone to steal from the neighboring tribes.

It was apparent to Kit that the stealing was done for fun rather than need. Kit had no problem gathering up the stolen property and returning it to the rightful owners. Kit felt the

Navajo people were happy to return the property as it gave them more to steal next time.

Kit had the Indian problem pretty well under control when Abraham Lincoln became President. Shortly after his inauguration, trouble between the North and South started. In June of 1861, Kit resigned his position as Indian Agent in order to fight for the preservation of the Union during the Civil War.

Chapter 10
The Civil War
and After

The Indians, and in particular the Navajo tribe, were still causing some problems. In spite of these problems, Kit turned his attention to the problems with the Union. In July of 1861, Kit was given the rank of Lieutenant Colonel and placed in charge of the New Mexico Volunteers. Their orders were to protect the settlers from any Indian depredation. Since many Southerners had also migrated to the area, Kit was also responsible for quelling any problems they might cause.

Lieutenant Colonel Carson and his volunteers were sent to Albuquerque for training. While he was there, Josefa and the children came to be with him. When the training was over, Josefa and the children returned to Taos, accompanied by a platoon of Volunteers. Lieutenant Colonel Carson and the rest of his men followed. They continued on to Fort Craig in Colorado.

Another important event at this time concerned John C. Fremont. He had retired from the Army and was spending some time in Europe. When he heard of the problems in the States, he immediately offered his services. On his return, he was given the rank of Brigadier General and placed in charge of the Armies of the West. His headquarters were in St. Louis, Missouri.

Carson had now been promoted to Colonel. Shortly after their arrival at Fort Craig, the Confederated army started a march toward Albuquerque. At this point the Confederate and Union Armies were separated by the Rio Grande River. Colonel Carson and his men were ordered to cross the river and form the right flank with the Colorado Pikes Peak regiment.

After crossing the river and forming their ordered position, Carson observed a column of Confederate soldiers cutting across their front. They were trying to take a 24-pound Union cannon that had been causing them considerable grief. When the Confederates came within rifle range, Carson and his men fired a volley into their ranks. At the same time the 24-pounder released a shot that landed in the middle of the group. The Confederates rapidly decided that attack was not a good idea and retreated. They left many dead and wounded soldiers behind. That evening, Colonel Carson and his men were ordered to re-cross the river and return to Fort Craig. With Carson's normal luck, he came through the Battle of Valverde without a scratch.

Approximately a month after returning to Fort Craig, Colonel Carson received orders to return to Albuquerque. On arrival, he was directed to form the New Mexico Cavalry. When a regiment had been formed and trained, Colonel Carson and his men were sent to Fort Stanton. This Fort, located in present day Lincoln County, New Mexico, had been abandoned the previous year. The Fort was now in a deplorable condition. Anything that was movable had been removed. Only the walls were left standing. Without protection, the settlements, ranches, and farms in the area had been vacated.

Colonel Carson's orders were to get the troops settled and then take the field against the Apaches and Navajo Indians. When the fort was abandoned, these two tribes had conducted raids throughout the area. Colonel Carson felt there was a better way of settling the problem, but orders were orders. The one order that Colonel Carson disliked the most was that all men of the Mesclera Apache tribe were to be killed whenever contacted. The women and children were to be saved.

In addition to fighting Indians, Colonel Carson was having trouble at Fort Stanton. There was a great deal of unrest. A Doctor Whitlock, who was a close friend of Colonel Carson, had come to Fort Stanton and requested assignment to Carson's Command. Colonel Carson felt this was a great idea. However, Captain Clayton felt strongly that it was not. The story goes that, prior to joining the army, Captain Clayton had been running liquor to the various Indian encampments. Doctor Whitlock was aware of this activity and reported it to the authorities.

When these two men met, there were immediate words between them. The Captain ordered an apology from the Doctor. Doctor Whitlock refused to give him one, stating he could prove everything he had ever said. With that, the Captain demanded a duel. He left to go to his quarters to get his pistol. Since the argument had occurred jut outside the Fort Trading Post, the Doctor went inside grabbed a shotgun off of the wall and returned to the street to await the

Captain. When the Captain returned, they both fired at the same time. The Doctor was hit in the wrist, which shattered the bone and the stock of the shotgun. The Captain was hit in the chest just missing the heart.

The Captain's men carried him back to his quarters where he died shortly thereafter. The troopers under the Captain were extremely loyal to him. They returned to the trading post where they found the Doctor trying to bandage his wrist. The troopers wasted no time in completing what the Captain had started. The Doctor's body was dragged from the store and dumped in a ditch. The troopers then marched by with each man taking a shot at the body.

When Carson heard about the incident he ordered the entire regiment to form up on the parade grounds. He then ordered the Captain's regiment to be disarmed and placed in the stockade. He assured them that they would all hang by sunset. Luckily, cooler minds talked Carson into releasing most of the prisoners and holding only the ringleaders. The troops that were released were turned over to civilian authorities for further legal processing.

When problems at Fort Stanton were brought under control, Colonel Carson took to the field against the Mescalero and Gila Apaches.

A major objective was to capture Mangas Colorados. Colonel Carson was never quite sure of the basic reason for this campaign. He felt the real reason was to gain the Apache territory that contained valuable mineral deposits. During this campaign, Mangas Colorados was killed along with his son and brother. In addition, approximately 60 warriors were slain.

When the war against the Apache Indians was considered complete, Carson was granted leave to return the Taos for rest and relaxation. While Carson was still at Taos, a Colonel Chavez arrived at Fort Wingate to start a campaign against the Navajo people.

During the summer of 1863, the Navajo chiefs were called to Santa Fe to sign a peace agreement. The chiefs came but were fully armed. When no peace agreement could be negotiated, a messenger was sent to Taos to locate Colonel Carson. When Carson was located he was presented with orders. He was to amass an army and proceed to the center of the Navajo Nation. This army was to be of sufficient strength to protect his troops, a supply depot, and hospital that was to be built. Carson assembled an army of approximately 750 men and proceeded to Pueblo Colorado. Here they established a Post called Fort Canby.

The Fort was named after General Canby, who was Carson's superior at the battle of Valverde. As soon as the fort was established Carson was ordered to start a vigorous campaign against the Navajo people. To accomplish this mission he was granted permission to use Ute warriors as trackers and spies.

While the Navajo men were not as good fighters as the Apache warriors, they more than held their own. At the start of the war, another problem was discovered. The Navajo people had no central government. Each family unit acted on its own. A promise made by one family was not binding to any other family. There was one major exception, all grain fields, gardens, and orchards were community property. Colonel Carson soon realized that the only way to subdue to Navajo people was to starve them out. With this knowledge, he ordered his men to destroy all grain fields, gardens, and orchards. The stored grain was taken to feed the army horses. Livestock was also taken, along with any stored vegetables.

After all food supplies that could be found were destroyed, Carson started a campaign to hunt the Navajo people. He was to gather all Navajo people that he could and send then to the Bosque Redondo Reservation which was located in central New Mexico. At the Bosque Redondo the women and children were to be educated to the white man's culture.

During the summer and fall of 1863, Carson had very little success in finding Navajo people. It appeared that they had all fled the country. The one thing that Carson did accomplish was a greater knowledge and understanding of the Southwest terrain.

During December and January Carson took his troops to the Canyon de Chelly. He felt this was the most likely place to find the Navajo people. The Canyon de Chelly is about 12 miles long with steep cliffs on both sides. A stream runs down the center with abundant grass on the valley floor. Colonel Carson posted troops at each end of the canyon to stop any possible Navajo escape. It wasn't long before an old Navajo man came into Carson's camp holding a white flag. He told Carson that his people were starving and that they would go peacefully to Pueblo Redondo if that was what was required. Carson gave him five days to gather his people and return to his camp.

Right on time the old man returned with 60 Navajo people. About the same time Carson started getting word that many others wanted to surrender. However, they were afraid to do so as they were sure this was a war of extermination. When they heard this was not true, they started to assemble. By the time Carson returned to Fort Canby he had about 3,000 Navajo people in custody. The Navajo were then marched to Santa Fe and then on to the Bosque Redondo.

On arrival at the Bosque Redondo there was an immediate problem. The Government, in all of their wisdom, felt that the Bosque Redondo was an ideal place for both the Navajo and Apache Indians. They both came from the same area of the Southwest and both spoke essentially the same language. This concept was far from the truth as the two tribes were mortal enemies.

Within a year problems were expanding at Bosque Redondo. The Apaches had all fled the area. The Navajo had stayed and were being urged to plant crops. They experienced one crop failure after another. During the winter of 1864-65 many hundreds of the Navajo died of starvation. It wasn't until 1867 that the Navajo people were released. Their care was transferred from the Department of the Army to the Bureau of Indian Affairs.

During the fall of 1864, Colonel Carson was ordered to bring the Kiowa and Comanche Indians under control. The plains Indians were causing havoc with the settlers and the wagon trains. Carson's first step was to recruit some 60 Apache and Ute scouts. The scouts soon found that the Kiowa and Comanche Indians were working out of Adobe Walls, an area in the Texas Panhandle.

With this information, Carson ordered his men to travel down the Canadian River toward Adobe Walls. When they were about 30 miles from Adobe Walls, Carson called a halt. This gave the troopers time to care for their horses, eat, and get some rest. On the following day, the troops started moving again. When they were about 15 miles from Adobe Walls, Apache scouts told Carson that the Indian warriors were approaching and were going to attack. At the top of a small hill, Carson stopped and placed his men in battle formation.

When the Kiowa and Comanche warriors approached, their strength was estimated at approximately 1,200 to 1,400. When the Indians started to attack, Carson ordered a cannon he had brought along to fire. The approaching Indians stopped in amazement. This cannon was something they had not bargained for, and they quickly fled the area.

When Colonel Carson returned from the battle of Adobe walls, he was granted a long overdue leave. As soon as possible, Carson returned to Taos to be with Josefa and their five children. He was able to stay in Taos until May of 1865. At that point the Plains Indians had started another vigorous campaign against the settlers and wagon trains. It was now necessary to send a military escort along with each wagon train.

In May, Carson was ordered to establish a camp at Cedar Springs on the Cimarron Trail.

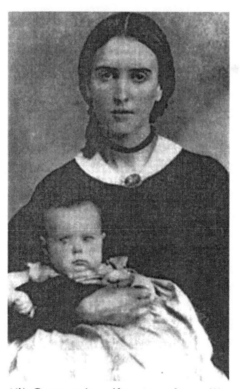

Kit Carson's wife, Josefa, with
their son, Kit Junior

Cedar Springs is located in the Panhandle of present day Oklahoma. He was to assist wagon trains traveling that route. When the assignment was made, Carson was promoted from Colonel to Brevet Brigadier General.

Shortly after the camp was established and the troops settled, Carson was called to serve on a special treaty commission. The commission was set up by the President. General Carson soon found that his views of Indian problems were not shared by the rest of the commission. The other members were strictly against smoking a peace pipe with any tribal leaders. Carson felt that this was the only way to hear their side of the problem, and not to do so was the root cause of the unrest. Another area of disagreement was in the establishment of a reservation. Carson felt that each tribe should have an area that they could call their own.

After this meeting, Kit Carson was called to the Office of President Andrew Johnson. Here the President signed the papers confirming his appointment as Brevet Brigadier General. This, however, was a short- lived honor as he was appointed Commander of Fort Garland. With this appointment his rank was reduced to Lieutenant Colonel. This didn't seem to bother Carson as he had greater interest in the job

Andrew Johnson
President of the United States 1865-1869

than he did in the rank. At Fort Garland, Kit was responsible for maintaining peace with the Colorado tribes. He was also responsible for seeing that no liquor was delivered to the native population.

When Carson went to Fort Garland, he took Josefa and their five children with him. It wasn't long before General Sherman came to visit. They were soon joined by Governor Cummings and General Rusling. Their objective was to arrange a meeting with the Utes. More specifically, they wanted the Ute Head Chief Ourey to be present. The objective of the meeting was for the Utes to settle on a reservation. The meeting was arranged with Carson acting as mediator. The Governor and Generals were amazed with Kit's fluency in Spanish and the Ute language. They also noted that when he spoke in English, he often hesitated while seeking the proper word.

In 1867, the U. S. Army was reducing their ranks. In the fall of that year, Brevet Brigadier General Carson was mustered out of the service. The years of Indian battles and the Civil War had taken their toll on Kit Carson's health. In addition, several years earlier, a horse Kit was riding had slipped and fallen on him. While Kit swore that no damage had been done, his labored breathing indicated otherwise.

Chief Ouray and Chipeta
Leader of the Ute tribe's Uncompahgre band

In the early spring of 1868, Kit was asked to come to Washington and help negotiate a new treaty with the Utes. The Government wanted to establish the exact location of the Ute reservation. Kit went to Washington partly at the urging of Josefa. She wanted him to see medical specialists while he was back there. Kit completed the work for the Ute people. He then visited the medical specialists that Josefa requested. The result of these visits was that there was very little hope for him to recover his health. The one bright spot of the trip was being met by his old friend, General Fremont.

Kit rested for several days before starting the long trip back to Denver. In Denver, Kit was met by Josefa, who traveled with him back to their new home at Bogsville on the Purgatoire River. On April 13, 1868, Josefa gave birth to a baby girl. Josefa passed away ten days after the delivery. One can only assume that the rigors of childbirth, her traveling and her advancing age were contributing factors in her death.

With the death of Josefa, Kit's health seemed to deteriorate. He was transported to the Army Hospital at Fort Lyons. On May 23, 1868, Kit passed into the next world, at the age of 59.

Kit's body was placed in a homemade casket and awarded full military honors. His body was transported by military escort about two miles from the Fort where his body was turned over to the family. The family took the body a short distance to Bogsville, where it was laid to rest beside Josefa. One can only hope that they are now together strolling through eternity.

Christopher "Kit" Carson
Last photograph of Christopher "Kit" Carson.
Taken in Boston in March 1868, two months
before his death.

Chapter 11
Epilogue

Genealogy

The following is a brief summation of the Carson family genealogy. Kit's grandfather, William Carson, was born in 1720 in Brandwich, Devonshire, England. In his youth he migrated to America and settled in North Carolina. In 1751, he married Eleanor McDuff. Their first child was Lindsey Carson. Lindsey would later become Kit Carson's father. In 1782, Lindsey married Lucy Bradley. The couple soon had four children. Shortly after the birth of the fourth child, Lindsey loaded his family into a wagon and took the Wilderness Road to Kentucky. It wasn't long before Lucy had another daughter. Shortly thereafter, Lucy died. Two years later, Lindsey married Rebecca Robinson. Rebecca and Lindsey Carson had six children together, one of which was Christopher Houston (Kit) Carson. When Kit came into the world he joined his parents and ten brothers and sisters in a one room log cabin. The cabin was located on Tate Creek in Madison County, Kentucky.

The Arapahoe Mystery

When Kit was about 25 years old, he married a young Arapahoe girl. They had one child, a daughter that was named Waa Nibi which literally translates into Singing Wind. Several references state that the child died at the age of two, and the mother shortly after that. Other references state that the child did not die.

When the daughter was about two, Kit took her to the old family homestead in Missouri. The homestead was now vacated. Kit took his daughter on to St. Louis where he did find a brother that had married and settled there. Kit paid the brother an agreed upon amount to see that the little girl was properly raised and educated. It can be assumed that his frequent trips to St. Louis were not to visit old friends, but rather to see his daughter and check on her well-being.

The probable reason for the secrecy was the feeling by the white population against half-breed children. This animosity was particularly strong in the eastern part of America.

Illiteracy

As stated in the text of the book, Kit Carson was never able to attend school and learn to read and write. At one point Kit stated that he didn't see the need to learn. He felt that learning to read and write would not improve his ability to track a man or animal. Neither would it improve his ability to shoot his rifle or pistol.

To the writer's knowledge, the first time the need did arise was after he became an Indian Agent. At this point he found that he had to make out reports. However, he was able to find help at the agency, primarily from his clerk. The Author could find no evidence that Kit ever had instructions in reading and writing. It is possible that with his agile mind he would be able to pick up some reading skills.

Reports attributed to Kit, and presumably written in later years, have perfect English, spelling, and punctuation. It seems almost inconceivable that Kit could attain these skills after years on the frontier.

The Navajo Long Walk

The forced march of the Navajo people from current day Fort Defiance to Santa Fe to the Bosque Redondo in New Mexico was a walk of approximately 1,200 miles. Due to lack of food, many of the Navajo people died of starvation along the way. The current day Navajo people have made this a historical trail and marked its path along the way.

References

The following References were used throughout the text to establish an outline of Kit Carson's life, and to obtain the details of his adventures. The Internet was used where additional information was desired pertaining to people, places, or events.

1. Time Life Books, *The Trail Blazers*, New York, New York, 1973

2. M. Morgan Estergreen, *Kit Carson: A Portrait in Courage*, U. Of Oklahoma Press, 1962

3. Noel Bertram Gerson, *Kit Carson, Folk Hero and Man*, Double Days Publishers, Garden City, New York, 1964

4. *Kit Carson's Autobiography*, Edited by Milo Milton Quaife, U. Of Nebraska Press, 1966

5. Time Life Books, *The Soldiers*, New York, New York, 1973

6. Bernice Blackwelder, *Great Westerner, The Story of Kit Carson*, Caxton Printers, Caldwell, Idaho, 1962

The map on pages 62–63 is from *Kit Carson: A Portrait in Courage*, by M. Morgan Estergreen. Copyright ©1962 by the University of Oklahoma Press, Norman. Reprinted by permission of the publisher. All Rights Reserved.

CPSIA information can be obtained at www.ICGtesting.com
Printed in the USA
BVOW08s0240060314

346819BV00001B/2/P